# FRENCH GARDENS
## A GUIDE

# FRENCH GARDENS
## A GUIDE

## BARBARA ABBS
Photographs by Deirdre Hall
Maps by Susan Rowland

Sagapress, Inc.
Sagaponack, New York

First published in 1994 by
The Gryphon Press, Lewes, England
Text copyright Barbara Abbs 1994
Photographs copyright Deirdre Hall 1994
Maps copyright Susan Rowland 1994

Every care has been taken to ensure that all the information in
this book is accurate. The publisher cannot accept any
responsibility for any errors that may appear or their consequences.

Library of Congress
Catalog Card Number 95-67047
Published in North America in 1995 by Sagapress, Inc.

Sagapress, Inc.
P.O. Box 21
Sagaponack, NY 11962

Manufactured in the United States of America

Front cover: La Roche-Courbon

## Introduction

For ease of reference France has been divided into four sections, North, the Paris Region, the Centre and the South. Within those broad areas, the regions, departments and gardens are listed alphabetically. Alpes Maritimes is arranged slightly differently.

Each garden is marked on a map but also has directions on how to find it and a reference to the Michelin Road Atlas given in the text. Paris is the exception. It is assumed that any visitor will have a street map of the city where the parks are clearly marked. Metro Stations are given only. The opening hours are as accurate as possible at the time of going to press but if a special journey is to be made to visit a garden, a telephone call to confirm the times of opening is strongly advised. Many of the owners speak English and most will open outside the stated hours, particularly for groups, if arrangements are made in advance.

Entrance charges (marked **E**) are for gardens only where possible and are banded into Inexpensive, below 20Fr; Moderate, between 21Fr and 50Fr and Expensive above that.

Many private gardens open to the public sometime in June and in particular during the first weekend of the month. Gardens opening on the Journées des Porte d'Ouverte are listed in leaflets produced by each region under the over-all direction of the Ministère de l'Equipement et du Logement, the Ministère de la Culture et de la Communication and the Secrétariat d'Etat à l'Environment. The lists should be available at the local Syndicat d'Initiative or Office du Tourisme. While the open days in June are for gardens, there is a similar day in September for architecture which is also a good opportunity to see gardens not normally open to the general public.

# THE REGIONS OF FRANCE

# CONTENTS

KEY TO MAPS

● Schoppenwihr - Garden

◉ STRASBOURG -
Town with garden(s)

☐ COLMAR -
Town with no garden

*BAS-RHIN* Departement

▬▬▬ Region

7

# NORTHERN FRANCE

## ALSACE

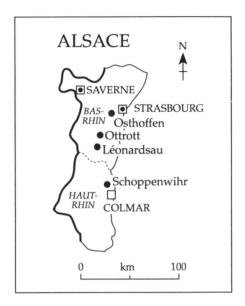

ALSACE    N

■ SAVERNE

BAS- ● ◙ STRASBOURG
RHIN   Osthoffen
    ● Ottrott
    ● Léonardsau

      ● Schoppenwihr
HAUT-  ▢
RHIN  COLMAR

0      km      100

**BAS RHIN**

CHATEAU DE LA LEONARDSAU
67210 Obernai. Tel: 88 95 64 13 (Office du tourisme)

*Obernai is 30 km south west of Strasbourg. Léonardsau is 3 km from the centre of Obernai. Take the D426, the route du vin, towards Ottrott. In Ottrott turn north to the D35 towards Rosheim. Léonardsau is on the east.(61 D1)* **Opening hours:** *Every day, 9-6. E. Free.*

Although the estate of Léonardsau, originally known as the Collegial de Saint-Leonard, has existed since the seventeenth century, the château that is there now was built in the first decades of this century by collector and painter, Albert de Dietrich. It became the property of the town of Obernai in 1970 and now houses the Musée du Cheval et de l'Attelage (horse and harness).

Around the château is an English style park with many fine conifers including *Pinus wallichiana*. The trees are frequently labelled. On one side of the château there is a *jardin à la française*. On other sides of the building there are a Japanese garden and an Italian garden with an entrance guarded by two stone lions. Statues, balls and domes of clipped box surround a stone *bassin* with a fountain.

## OSTHOFFEN
67990 Osthoffen. Tel: 88 96 00 23.

*15 km west of Strasbourg. Take the N4 to Saverne and after the village of Ittenheim, take the first road on the left. Osthoffen is 2 km past the village of Handschduheim.(43 D4)* **Opening hours:** *Saturday and Sunday 3-6. E. Free.*

Osthoffen is a picturesque moated château with roofs of the patterned yellow and green glazed tiles common to this part of the country. The derelict outbuildings at the rear of the château are covered with *Parthenocissus henryana* and vines cascade over other walls and around the moat. There are some clipped yews along the edge of the moat and in the courtyard and the site is surrounded by a wooded park. In the course of restoration.

## FOYER DE CHARITE
Foyer de Charité, 51 rue Principale, 67530 Ottrott. Tel: 88 95 81 27.

*South west of Strasbourg. Leave Strasbourg by the D392 which passes the airport, then take the N422 to Obernai. Turn right towards Obernai but stay on the by-pass, D426 and continue to Ottrott. The Foyer de Charité is in the centre of the town. (61 D1). The park, attached to the Foyer, which is a centre for retreats, is virtually open all the time. Visitors should call at the Secretariat in the main building first. E. Free. Wheelchairs, most parts accessible.*

The park is being developed as a promenade for contemplation and meditation for those who come here on retreat.

The trees are well-labelled: there are American and red oaks, gleditsia, *Chamaecyparis nootkatensis, Maclura pomifera,* a *Pterocarya fraxinifolia,* all of good size. There are new plantings of *Caragana arborescens, Corylopsis sinensis, Celtis bungeana* and *Zelkova schneideriana,* as well as shrubs like rhamnus, syringa and callicarpa. In the autumn, the meadow around which most of the trees are planted, is studded with colchicums.

There is a tiny area of formal garden to the right of the Foyer, with statues and stone from an earlier building; also a redoubt and the twelfth century chapel of St Nicholas, a pond and boggy area, planted with willows, rhododendrons and lively with marsh marigolds.

## SAVERNE ROSERAIE
Route de Paris, 67700 Saverne. Tel: 88 71 83 33.

*West of the château on the N4 Route de Paris, to Sarrebourg. (42 C3)* **Opening hours:** *3 June to 10 September, 9-7. E. Inexpensive. Toilets.*

This very French style rose garden is run, with great enthusiasm by a group of volunteers, the 'Friends of the Rose of Alsace and Lorraine'. The roses are mainly hybrid teas, cluster roses and climbers that will flourish in the severe climate of Alsace, but also new varieties that participate in the 'International Concours' of roses. The roses are well labelled.

JARDIN BOTANIQUE, COL DE SAVERNE
67700 Saverne. Tel: 88 91 10 14.

*3 km west of Saverne on the N4 to Sarrebourg. Good parking on the opposite side of the road. (42 C3).* **Opening hours:** *May to mid-September, Monday to Friday, 9-5; Sundays and holidays, 2-6. July -August, as above but Saturday, Sunday and holidays 2-7. E. Inexpensive.*

This extremely pleasant botanic garden, like the Roseraie in the town, is run by a dedicated group of volunteers. The garden is in a clearing on the side of the Col de Saverne and the beds are cut out of the hillside.

The plants are grouped in geographical areas and a number of plants that are rare in Alsace and the Vosges such as martagon lilies, anemones and aconites, are to be found here. The orchid collection is especially fine with more indigenous orchids than can be found anywhere else, (almost 20 species) and there are also orchid trial grounds. Beneath the many attractive conifers are an alpine garden, a dry rock garden, a calcareous rock garden, a marsh with carnivorous plants, a collection of ferns, one of peonies and a section for ericaceous plants.

The garden is at its best in May and June, with many different saxifrages on the large rock garden in flower, and the rhododendrons and azaleas blooming, but the plants are so various that there are always many in flower. In mid-September for example, *Acer tataricum ginnala* was beginning to turn red; the brilliant rose-crimson flowers of *Callirhoë involucrata* were lighting up the rock garden, accompanied by *Dianthus superbus* and the dusty brownish pink *Apios americana* (cinnamon vine). The pale yellow flowers of *Aristolochia clematitis, Salvia glutinosa* and *Diervilla lonicera* gleamed in the late summer sun.

The far end of the garden is planted with trees,shrubs and conifers including nothofagus, *Cunninghamia lanceolata Hydrangea aspera villosa* and *Amorpha fruticosa*, (false indigo). *Veratrum nigrum* seeds everywhere, as do several digitalis species. This is an attractive garden, full of interest and variety.

JARDIN BOTANIQUE DE STRASBOURG
28 rue Goethe, 67083 Strasbourg. Tel: 88 35 83 67.

*A difficult city to drive in! A simple way to travel is to go round the ring road, Quai Louis Pasteur, towards Place de l'Etoile. Don't cross the canal to the Place, but keep*

10

*straight on around the quays, beyond the Parc de la Citadelle. Turn left at Pont d'Anvers along Avenue de la Foret Noire. The Church of St Maurice and then the Place Arnold are on the right, the Botanic Gardens on the left, in the Rue Goethe opposite. Buses 2, 7 and 32. (43 E9)* **Opening hours:** *All year, week days 8-12 and 2-5; March to September, open on Sunday, 8-12; closed on Saturday all year. E. Free. Wheelchairs. Toilets in the building.*

An attractively laid out botanic garden set around two large buildings, the old circular observatory and the modern Institute of Botany of the University Louis Pasteur.

To the left of the entrance is a small lake, surrounded by rushes, gunnera and weeping willows. Beyond that are experimental trial grounds bordered by groups of rosaceae, walnut and birch trees. On the other side of the lake is a bed of plants from New Zealand, containing hebes and olearias in variety. There is also a collection of bamboos. Outside the institute building is a plunge bed, where plants from the cold greenhouse are plunged in sand during the summer. On the other side of the tropical glasshouse are a mediterranean rock garden, an alpinum and a bed of 'useful' plants such as medicinal herbs, dye and oil producing plants.

An old round greenhouse (1884) contains a pool with water lilies and other tropical plants. Palm trees, cycads, papyrus, banana and bromeliads grow in a tropical house while a cold house has citrus trees, *Acca sellowiana*, carob and acacia. Another house contains cacti and succulents.

Another area with informally shaped beds and winding paths, contains asters, magnolias and various monocotyledons. Many flowering trees and shrubs flourish in the garden: medlars and tree peonies, cistus and camellias. There are collections of lime-hating plants and plants that flourish in sand such as gorse, broom, pine trees and a coarse grass known as oyat. A large *Pterocarya fraxinifolia* dates from the nineteenth century but this is dwarfed by a *Carya illinoinensis* (pecan). It is 40 m high and still growing.

PARC DE L'ORANGERIE
Avenue de l'Europe, 67000 Strasbourg.

*Opposite the Palais de l'Europe. From the Jardin Botanique, return to Place Arnold, cross and drive straight up rue de Verdun and into the car park. (43 E9)* **Opening hours:** *permanently. E. Free. Wheelchairs. Toilets. Restaurant.*

This *parc à l'anglaise* contains some good trees and shrubs. The orangery itself is called the Pavillon Josephine after the Empress Josephine who stayed in Strasbourg. It was erected to house some orange trees that came from a château destroyed in the Revolution and is surrounded by beds of herbaceous plants.

Most of the flowers in the park are bedding plants but they are particularly well laid out. A spectacular waterfall cascades from a rocky mound in the middle of a large lake. There are fine *allées*, a gastronomic restaurant and games areas for children. The zoo in the park has an area of high trees and pillars that is inhabited by a colony of storks.

JARDIN GOTHIQUE
Musée de l'Oeuvre Notre-Dame, 3 Place du Château, 67000 Strasbourg.

*At the side of the cathedral by the modern art museum. Follow signs to Cathedral and Musée de l'Oeuvre Notre Dame. Access through the museum. (43 E9)* **Opening hours:** *1 April to 31 October, 10-12 and 2-6; 1 November to 30 March, 2-6. Closed on Tuesdays and holidays. Wheelchairs. Toilets close by (and also in museum).*

This tiny shaded mediaeval garden can be seen quite well from outside - there are grilles in the walls on two sides. It was created in 1937 and modelled on gardens of the fifteenth century and will be of particular interest to historians. A tiny shaded area is divided into three: one section has a tiny stream, a lime tree and an octagonal *bassin* which is actually a baptismal tank; a central section contains nine square beds planted with medicinal and other herbs; a third area is grassed and has a plane tree and beech trees and another circular baptismal tank. On the walls are statues and ancient plaques.


**HAUT RHIN**

PARC DE SCHOPPENWIHR
68000 Colmar. Tel: 89 41 22 37.

*6 km north of Colmar clearly signed on the N83 to Strasbourg. Easy to find from Strasbourg, but from Colmar, take the first road to the right after the airport, turn right to go under the N83, then right again. ((61 D3)* **Opening hours:** *Every day, 1 April to 11 November, 10-12 and 2-6.* **E.** *Very moderate. Toilets. Wheelchairs.*

Schoppenwihr is a wooded park in the romantic English style. An avenue of planes leads to the new farmhouse, the outbuildings and the ruins of the old château.

The moat that surrounded the old château was extended to form a *miroir d'eau*, the *allée* of plane trees planted and the *cour d'honneur* arranged by Achille Duchêne in between the two world wars. The *miroir d'eau* has lost its function but not its beauty. The surface mirrors nothing but is thickly covered with luminous pale green duckweed through which a swan occasionally carves a stately path.

The ruins of the old château are still there overlooking the moat and are planted with prostrate conifers, cotoneaster, rosemary and a large contorted willow.

In about 1750 Schoppenwihr was a simple, middle class house surrounded by water and with access by a small bridge. The greater part of the park was forested. However the manor house of the eighteenth century was completely remodelled in the nineteenth, transformed into a sumptuous château, while the park was also altered and turned into a *parc à l'anglaise* by a Scottish architect. Rare trees were planted - taxodium, ginkgo and sophora - and the river was turned into a small stream with lakes, bridges and tiny islands. All this occurred when the owner's sister became a lady-in-waiting to the Empress Eugenie and the château became a centre of high society. Glasshouses were constructed and filled with orchids, orange trees and palms, while fêtes and fireworks were organised to amuse the Russian grand dukes, the Austrian archdukes and others who were guests here.

Two world wars destroyed the château. Several months after the Liberation in World War II, mines exploded, damaging the already ravaged building beyond repair. Schoppenwihr has become a working farm again, but still has the attractively planted ruins, the *parc anglais* and a recently restored romantic feature of fallen columns on one of the islands, the Ile de Demoiselles.

In spite of its important history, Schoppenwihr is under threat of development from the local authority. Visitors making their way through the narrowentrance road, by a sawmill and the tiny shacks of 'guest workers' cannot fail to be aware of the encroaching industrial zone, the airport, the Route National and the railway. Yet there is pressure to expand the industrial zone even further.

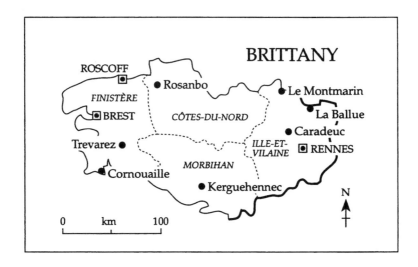

## COTES DU NORD

CHATEAU DE ROSANBO
22420 Lanvellec. Tel: 96 35 18 77.

*Leave the N12 expressway between St-Brieuc and Morlaix at exit Begarc'hra, Plouaret to D11, and2 then take left turn to Rosanbo Lanvellec.(27 F2)* **Opening hours:** *Sundays and holidays ,1 April to 15 June and 15 September to 31 October, 2-5.30; 15 to 30 June and 1to 15 September, every day 2-5.30. 1 July to 31 August, every day, 10.30-6.30. E. Moderate. Wheelchairs. Toilets. Café.*

The seventeenth century château has an interesting formal French garden of terraces and lawns, divided by arbours and clipped hedges into green rooms. One of the 'rooms' is a salon of the four seasons, another an open air theatre. There are statues of cherubs and lions, a semi-circular *bassin* in front of the château and a long green tunnel to one side. The surrounding park has long *allées* shaded by arching hornbeams known as Les Charmilles, said to be from a design by Le Nôtre.

## FINISTERE

CONSERVATOIRE BOTANIQUE, BREST
52 Allée du Bot, 29200 Brest. Tel: 98 02 63 14. Fax: 98 41 88 95.

*To the east of the town centre. The Vallon du Stang Alar in which the Conservatoire Botanique is situated is at the end of the Allée du Bot. **Opening hours:** Every day, in summer 9-8; winter 9-6. E. Free. Wheelchairs. Toilets.*

The Conservatoire Botanique is a conservation area rather than a garden, but sited in a picturesque valley, the Vallon du Stang Alar with several large lakes, linked by rushing streams. It is dedicated to the preservation of endangered flowering plants from both temperate and warmer countries - the latter in some of the 1000 sq.m. of glasshouse.

The 35 ha valley is divided into a public park and the conservation area and contains a wide variety of habitats - marsh and cliff face, wood and meadow - where endangered species can be grown in as natural a way as possible.

There is also a gene bank, a library and an information centre for visitors. The Conservatoire sees its function not only as preserving flowering plants but also as educating the public about conservation. Sixty thousand plants, that is one in four, are threatened with imminent extinction.

JARDIN BOTANIQUE DE CORNOUAILLE
Combrit, 29120 Pont l'Abbé. Tel: 98 56 44 93 and 98 87 34 56 for reservations.

*On the D44 between Pont l'Abbé and Benodet at Combrit. (44 C3) **Opening hours:** May, June and September, every day 10-12 and 2-7; July and August, every day 10-7; March, April, October, Sundays 2-6. E. Moderate. Wheelchairs.*

The first plantings here were made in 1983. Since then there have been unusually cold winters, the hurricane of 1987 and more recently, droughts. M. Gueguen, who with his family, owns and runs the garden, worked at Hilliers and has a real knowledge of and feel for plants. and is succeeding in creating an interesting garden despite these setbacks.

The plants in this botanic garden are well labelled and there are comprehensive collections of shrubs and trees: 250 acers, 50 viburnums, 30 different cornus, 80 ilex, 75 prunus and such magnolias as *M. tripetala, M. hypoleuca, M. x wiesneri, wilsonii* and *M. sieboldii sinensis.*

The glory of the garden is its rhododendrons. With 420 different species and varieties there is color almost all year, beginning in February and reaching a peak in May and June. There are *R. decorum, R. fortuneii* and *R. fortuneii discolor,* many hybrids from Exbury, the whole series of Loderi varieties as well as the tender species *R. formosum* and *R. maddenii crassum.* In June the 300 species and old roses flower, while later, fuchsias, hydrangeas and dahlias give way to the autumn color of the acers, stewartias and styrax. A camellia walk has such unusual varieties as the yellow *Camellia nitidissima nitidissima* together with *C. cheirangulosa, C. caudata* and *C. 'Zig-zag'.*

Among the indigenous growth of oak and pine grow *Tetradium danielii hupehensis, Cupressus torulosa* 'Cashmiriana' and *C. duclouxiana, Eleutherococcus sieboldianus* and *Lomatia ferruginea*. Some of the original trees are used as supports for climbers like *Rosa filipes, Hydrangea anomala petiolaris* and *Smilax hispida*. A rock garden is in the making and two lakes, already richly alive with wild plants, will have lotus, waterlilies, primulas and iris added.

MAISON ROUGE
Roc'h Hievec 29211 Roscoff.

*Close to the ferry port. Well signed. **Opening hours:** All the time. **E.** Free. Wheelchairs, much is accessible.*

This exotic garden of sub-tropical plants around a natural rock outcrop overlooking the bay of Morlaix is the result of a collaboration between the local authority and the town horticultural society. Date palms are underplanted with agaves, aloes and phormiums and in the summer tender bedding plants in brilliant colors are massed in between. Varieties of osteospermum and euryops flourish in the benign climate.

CHATEAU DE TREVAREZ
29163 St Goazec.

*North east of Quimper. Drive for 21 km along the D15 to Coray, then north on the D36 for 14 km. Well signed. (45 E1) **Opening hours:** 1 April to 30 June and 1 to 30 September every day except Tuesday, 1-7; 1 July to 31 August, every day 11-7; 1 October to 31 March, Saturday, Sunday and holidays 2-6. **E.** Inexpensive to moderate, according to displays. Toilets. Wheelchairs.*

A large park planted with rare trees and many hundreds of rhododendrons, azaleas and camellias surrounds the château of Trevarez. The château was built at the beginning of the century by an ambitious President of the General Council of the Department of Finistère, James de Kerjégu. He did not, alas, live long to enjoy it. In World War II it was occupied by the Germans and then bombed by the RAF. Happily, however, it was acquired in 1968 by the Department of Finistère itself and the ornamental gardens were opened to the public in 1971.

In August and September there are festivals of dahlias, hydrangeas and fuchsias which add another season of interest for flower lovers in addition to the great spring display of camellias.

Like many other Brittany gardens, Trevarez suffered in the hurricane of 1987, losing 60 per cent of its trees and many of the shrubs and flowers. As in England however, plans were soon put in hand to use the opportunity of replanting to give the garden a new lease of life. A garden *à la française*, a bulb collection, and water gardens with aquatic plants were planned, to further extend the flowering season of the garden. Magnolias, oaks and maples have also been added to the park.

## ILLE ET VILAINE

LA BALLUE
35560 Bazouges-la-Pérouse. Tel: 45 48 78 90.

*East of Combourg.Take the D796 to Bazouges and Tremblay, turn left at Bazouges to the D90, then first right and right again. (48 C1) . **Opening hours:** 15 June to 15 October, every day, 11-12 and 2-7. This garden has recently changed hands and checking the opening hours is strongly advised. E. Moderate. Wheelchairs, part. Toilets.*

The rare baroque garden at La Ballue, part of which was originally created during the reign of Louis XIII, has been restored with the help of landscape architect Paul Maymont.

In front of the château is a classical *jardin à la française* with triangular beds and clipped yews around a hexagonal pool. Next to this traditional *parterre* is the *Jardin Baroque en Diagonale.* The large rectangular area is crossed by two diagonal paths which pass twelve different plantings or devices designed to amuse and surprise the visitor: a concept based on the Mannerist gardens of Italy, except that there, mechanical devices, like hidden fountains, were used to provide the 'surprise'. Among the surprises at La Ballue are a miniature botanic garden, a 'tormented' garden (with contorted hazel, beech and hawthorn); a scented grove containing gardenias, jasmine, tuberoses and *Hedychium gardnerianum*, a semi-circular open air theatre, a maze, a grove of camellias and roses and several arboreta. One arboretum contains trees with unusual bark, another 'extraordinary grafts' and a third, 'ancient giants'.

Behind the building is the *Verger Baroque en Pots,* an 'orchard' in which all the fruit trees, dwarf and miniature apples, cherries, pears and peaches, are cultivated in pots. There is an avenue of palm and orange trees, an *allée* of wisteria and a collection of magnolias. Altogether, the garden contains 5,000 trees and 60 rare shrubs.

Inside the château are several rooms dedicated to the History of Gardens. There are illustrations of gardens from ancient Egypt and Mesopotamia, from mediaeval Europe, from China and Japan as well as 'Follies' from as far apart as Sweden and Italy, and a collection of pottery fruit and flowers, bonsai and orchids.

## CHATEAU DE CARADEUC
35190 Bécherel. Tel: 45 48 78 90.

*From Rennes to Dinan take the main N137 and then the D27/D68/D2. Turn west at Bécherel, on to the D20. The château sits at the foot of a television mast that dominates the country for miles around. (48 A2).* **Opening hours:** *All year, 9-12.30 and 1.30 to sunset. E. Inexpensive. Wheelchairs, most parts accessible.*

The park at Caradeuc is described as the 'Breton Versailles' but Caradeuc is on a more comfortably domestic scale. Its statues and *fabriques* are not all of a piece like Versailles, but rather are examples of the art of serendipity.

The château was built about 1723 and the original garden was transformed into a park *à l'anglaise* in the nineteenth century. It was restored to a traditional French style at the end of that century by Edouard André the landscape architect who worked with Haussmann and Alphand on the Paris parks and boulevards.

The plan of the grounds is straightforward, with a main axis that begins in the car park, on the opposite side of the road outside the château with a statue of Cupid, and continues through a delightful gatehouse based on the pavilion at Bagatelle, then via a statue of Philemon beneath an arch of hornbeam to the château.

In front of the château is a symmetrical *jardin à la Française* with balustraded compartments, clipped yews, roses and ornamental ponds which reflect two Renaissance porticoes that were formerly the main entrance to a neighbouring château. The loveliest garden, the green shade-dappled, lyre-shaped Garden of Diana, is at right angles to the main drive, enclosed by English oaks and a hedge of clipped hornbeam.

Statues of all styles, different materials and from a variety of sources, are carefully placed within the design. Each statue has to be discovered, in its niche or arbour, limiting what is visible at any one time. This arrangement creates tranquillity yet gives a continuous sense of anticipation. A rounded Zephyr in warm brown wood stares down a side avenue; a larger than life statue of Louis XVI eternally opens the States General in a sombre corner. A mediaeval statue of Joan of Arc, hands tied behind her back and wearing a huge mitre, faces a classical figure of a child hunter across the Circus of Emperors. Other pleasures are a mound covered with day lilies, topped by a Japanese stone lantern, and an old granite cross on which the worn figure of Christ has each leg separately nailed, an indicator of great age.

The basic simplicity of the design and of the planting holds together the diversity of garden ornament, creating a garden of peaceful walks and *allées*, that is yet full of surprises. Go in the morning if you can and you may have it to yourself.

## LE MANOIR
Port de Roche, 35660 Langon. Tel: 99 08 75 55.

*Take the A137 south from Rennes. 20 km south of Bain de Bretagne, take exit for Le Grand Fougeray, follow signs for St Anne sur Vilaine and Renac. Follow D56 for 14 km to Port de Roche. Cross river and railway line.* **Opening hours:** *Every day, April to October, 11-5.* ***E.*** *Moderate. Refreshments.*

Alan Mason's television programs about his restoration of the garden at Le Manoir were very popular in England. Now the lovely Breton manor house and the garden with the ornamental lake, herbaceous borders, woodland garden, English-style lawn and French-style ornamental vegetable and herb garden has been given an accolade by the French and put in the Top 200 French Gardens to Visit.

Ancient oak trees give the garden an air of maturity, and it is planted for year round interest including a copse of *Ginkgo biloba* and *Nyssa sylvatica* for autumn color and camellias, azaleas and cyclamen for spring.

## LE MONTMARIN
35730 Pleurtuit. Tel: 99 88 58 79.

*10 km from St Malo. Take the road to Barrage de la Rance. After the Barrage, turn left at traffic lights. At Le Richardais take road to Le Minihic sur Rance. Le Montmarin is 2 km on the left.* **Opening hours:** *Guided visits, Mondays, at 3 from 15 June to 31 August. Large plant fairs, second week-ends of May and October.* ***E.*** *Moderate. Wheelchairs, most areas accessible. Toilets.*

The garden has a formal French *parterre,* a good herbaceous border with groups of alstroemeria and romneya, collections of euphorbias, hellebores, bulbs and a large area of heathers plus a fine terraced rock garden which follows the bank of the river Rance.

## JARDIN THABOR
Place Ste-Melaine, 35000 Rennes.

*North of N157 from Vitré and Laval, and south of N12 from Fougères, before the centre of the town, and just behind the Church of Notre Dame. Well signed. (48 C3)* **Opening hours:** *Every day 7-5.30 or until 9.30 according to season.* ***E.*** *Free. Wheelchairs. Toilets.*

Botanical gardens in provincial towns vary a good deal, but the Jardin Thabor is in the first rank. Like other public gardens, it also has carpet bedding, bandstand and children's play area.

The 10 ha park was designed by Denis Bühler in 1868 in his characteristic style: functional paths, lawns with clumps of trees of a single species, widely separated. A group of *Sequoiadendron gigantea* is a trade mark here. There is a picturesque area, *allées* of lime and chestnut; specimen trees including an ancient *Magnolia grandiflora*, a huge *Robinia pseudoacacia* with racemes of white pea flowers in June, the shrubby *Halesia carolina*, (snow-drop tree), and a gnarled *Quercus suber* (cork oak). Other features include a rose garden where rambler roses are grown in a variety of ways, a dahlia collection, topiary, a dovecote shaped like a pagoda, banks of rhododen-drons, camellia and pieris walks and, unusually for a French park, island beds with peonies, erigerons, cornflowers and day lilies. Everything is well labelled, and there are still the order beds to see.

These are attractively arranged in concentric circles round a central pool and ring of conifers. A circle of willows, poplars and sorbus - including *S.asplenifolia, S. latifolia and S. torminalis*, (wild service tree), follows and then, in ever increasing circles, families of herbaceous plants and shrubs, ending with an outer ring of hybrid tea roses.

## MORBIHAN

### CHATEAU DE KERGUEHENNEC
Bignan, 56500 Locmine. Tel: 97 60 44 44.

*North of Vannes on the D767. After the village of Meucon take the D778 to the right to St Jean de Brevelay, then the D1 to Bignan. In Bignan turn right to Kerguehennec. (47 D3)* **Opening hours:** *Every day except Monday, 10-6. E. Moderate. Wheel-chairs. Toilets.*

The Domaine de Kerguehennec is now a a Centre of Contemporary Art with exhibitions in the château and modern sculpture excitingly placed in the park. Pieces of sculpture by Richard Long and Ian Hamilton Finlay can be found there, among works by other contemporary European sculptors.

The château has changed hands many times since the land was noted as being owned by the Vicomte de Bignan in the fifteenth century. The present château was designed by one of the finest architects from Morbihan, Olivier Delourme, for a family of Swiss bankers and is set around an enormous courtyard with an elegant pool in the centre.

The park which surrounds the château was designed in 1872 by the Bühler brothers.The perspective to the south is preserved in its classical form. To the north is a vast lawn and the wood of fine trees - beeches, chestnuts and oaks (including *Quercus castaneifolia*, the chestnut leaved oak from the Caucasus).There are also liquidambars, American oaks, sequoias and cypresses. Amongst these trees pieces of modern sculpture are sited (one is even placed high in a tree) competing for interest with groups of rhododendrons, camellias and azaleas.

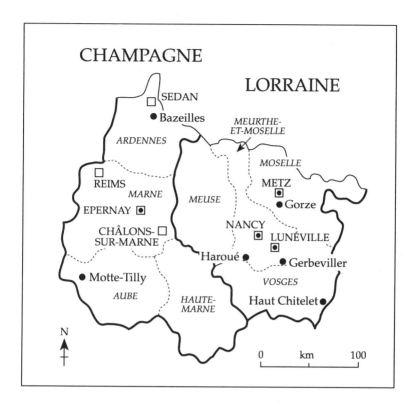

## ARDENNES

BAZEILLES
08140 Bazeilles. Tel: 24 27 09 68.

*3 km south of Sedan on the N43 to Montmedy turn right on to the D764. The stable block of the château is now a hotel and it is well signed. (21 F2).* **Opening hours:** *All year except for Monday 10-12 and 2-6.* **E.** *Free, exterior visits only. Wheelchairs - flat but thick gravel in places.*

Perhaps the young owners of the château will soon persuade the state to help with the restoration of this listed garden. A photograph on the brochure for the hotel shows how splendid the rear façade of the château looked reflected in one of the four rectangular pools that were such a feature of the formal garden. A fire in 1989 destroyed the right wing of the château and a project for its complete restoration including the pools, is under way.

21

There are some exceptionally good garden buildings: an orangery with a tiled roof and a curved front like the keel of a boat, two matching *pavillons d'amour* and, at the far end of the garden, in a corner, a *colombier* or dovecote. Some of the statues in the park are protected with polythene as are the statues on the front of the château.

The restoration of the garden is a priority for the owners now that the hotel is open and the orangery has become a restaurant. The château itself is the masterpiece of the architect Héré who was responsible for the Place Stanislas in Nancy.


## AUBE

### CHATEAU DE LA MOTTE-TILLY
10400  La Motte-Tilly. Tel: 25 39 84 54.

*5 km west of Nogent-sur-Seine on the D951 to Fontainebleau. (55 F2)* **Opening hours:** *April, May, June and September, every day except Tuesday, 10-11.45 and 2-6 (till 7 on Sundays and holidays in July and August); October and November, Saturday and Sunday 2-5. 30. E. Moderate. Toilets.*

The Château de la Motte-Tilly was built in 1754, but, as in so many cases, the eighteenth century formal gardens were replaced with an English style landscape park just before the Revolution. In 1910 the original garden to the north and south of the castle was restored.

The entrance is very imposing, with a semi-circular curved grille and two identical gatehouses. There is a long walk to a second gate and the *cour d'honneur* with its four, symmetrical, grass *parterres* and four small pavilions. The whole site is enclosed by large trees.

Behind the château, conical yews lead down to a lower terrace, then to the grand *miroir d'eau* bordered by double rows of limes, which extends to a long canal. The vista from the house is continued with an avenue of poplars planted in 1910 that stretches to the horizon. The gardens are very neatly kept and the great parterre was replanted in 1993 with yews and standard roses.


## MARNE

### JARDIN MOET ET CHANDON
Avenue de Champagne, 51200 Epernay

*Opposite the Moet et Chandon building in the Avenue de Champagne in the centre of Epernay. (38 A2)* **Opening hours:** *1 April to 31 October. Call at the 'Hall of Welcome', 18 Avenue de Champagne, and one of the hostesses will give directions.*

*No groups without prior written demand. E. Free*

A small, formally laid out garden surrounded by chestnut trees and with an elegant orangery reflected in a *miroir d'eau*.

No expense is spared here and every possible bedding plant in its biggest and brightest form is crowded into the narrow beds that outline the rectangular lawns. It is difficult to appreciate the orangery because of the distraction of particularly vivid mosaiculture.

Also in Epernay, the **Town Hall Garden** in the avenue de Champagne is equally remarkable.

The **Jardin d'Horticulture,** Rue du Comte de Lambertye, off the D51 out of the town, is a tiny park with topiary. Over a bridge is a small garden of labelled shrubs, conifers and trained fruit trees, black currants, peaches, plums, mirabelles, apples and pears. Ask the park keeper for the key.

# LORRAINE
Map: see page 21

## MEURTHE ET MOSELLE

LES BOSQUETS
54300 Lunéville. Tel: 83 73 18 27.

*The Bosquets is the garden of the château to the north of the town centre. It is well signed. (41 F4). Opening hours: Permanently open. E. Free. Wheelchairs. Toilets*

This historic garden, designed at the beginning of the eighteenth century and then extended by ex-King Stanislas of Poland, the father-in-law of Louis XV, has been municipalised in the worst possible way. Where there should be clipped box and yews, and fountains to give height, there are now bedding plants. Canna lilies, cleomes, French marigolds and *Salvia farinacea* all vie with each other to shriek the loudest.

CHATEAU DE GERBEVILLER
54830 Gerbeviller

*South east of Nancy and Lunéville. Take the D914 from Lunéville to Rambervillers and then turn into Gerbeviller, towards the Maison de Retraite. The single-storied château, rebuilt in 1920 after being burnt down during World War I, is tucked away behind a hedge, opposite its chapel. Opening hours: Saturday and Sunday 2-6. Groups welcomed. E. Inexpensive. Wheelchairs, part is accessible.*

On one side there is a pleasant wood surrounding a kitchen garden, on the other an open meadow with a river flowing through. Features include a rock garden and pond with waterlilies and two *fabriques*, of particular interest to garden historians.

At the end of the meadow is a delightful pink brick pavilion, the *Pavillon rouge*. Dating from the seventeenth century, the building has stone dressings and curved steps. Inside, the central room has a vaulted brick ceiling and niches in the walls, and two staircases, that intertwine but never meet.

At the edge of the woodland, overlooking the meadow, is an eighteenth century grotto with statues in niches and two flights of steps to the roof. The balustrades have elaborate narrow cascades down them. Inside, the grotto, or *nymphée*, is unusually spacious, and lined with shells, tufa and red and white stone chippings in what were once elaborate designs. The central room has a small basin in the shape of a shell set into each wall.

CHATEAU D'HAROUE
54740 Haroué. Tel. 83 52 40 14. Fax. 83 52 44 19.

*30 km south of Nancy on motorway in the direction of Epinal. Take the exit for Haroué. The village is 5km from the motorway and the château is in the centre. (59 E1)* **Opening hours:** *Every day 1 April to 11 November, 2-6.* **E.** *Gardens, moderate; guided tour of the château, and the gardens, moderate. Toilets. Wheelchairs. Cafeteria, week-ends only.*

Surprisingly there was no garden planned in the eighteenth century when the château was built although some trees were planted in what is called the Bosquet. The formal garden at the back of the château was designed by Emilio Terry in 1957 while the eight radiating *allées* and the central pool in the Bosquet, were created by Marc, Prince de Beauvau after he had inherited the estate in 1942. The attractive flower garden behind the stable courtyard was designed for the present owner's grandmother by Russell Page in 1952-53.

The formal garden at the rear of the château is remarkable for the liberal number of statues, regularly spaced and interspersed with clipped shrubs. The statues, although from the eighteenth century and of classical design, are unaccustomedly white and eyecatching. A narrow canal at the end of the garden, acts as a ha-ha and gives an uninterrupted view of the fields beyond.

The Russell Page garden fell into disrepair some years ago but has now been delightfully replanted by English designer, Cyndie Simon, in a scheme of pink, white and grey. Margaret Merrill roses, shrubs and herbaceous plants are framed in clipped box and hornbeam, against a background of a circular *colombier* of soft pink brick. The effect is very satisfying as is that of the stable courtyard, a simple square edged by pleached limes, divided into four, each quarter planted with a catalpa.

## JARDIN BOTANIQUE DU MONTET
100 rue du Jardin Botanique, 54600 Villers-lès-Nancy. Tel: 83 41 47 47.

*South west of the centrer of Nancy. Take the Avenue General Leclerc, D974 to Neufchateau and Dijon, (or Exit Chavigny, Nancy Sud-Ouest, from the A33 by-pass if you are coming into the city) and at the Velodrom, take the right turn into Boulevard des Aiguillettes. At the second traffic lights, turn left, through the University of Nancy Faculty of Science buildings. (41 D4). Bus: No.4, alight 'Victor Basch'; No.16, alight Lycée des biotechnologies. Opening hours: Every day, 2-5. Sundays and holidays from April to October, 2-6. E. Gardens free. Greenhouses, inexpensive. Toilets. Wheelchairs, parts are accessible. (A visit to the greenhouses may be arranged in advance.)*

The Jardin Botanique du Montet is another creation of the prodigious M. Pierre Valck, the Conservateur of the Conservatorie et Jardins Botanique de Nancy, and the moving spirit behind the alpine garden at Haut Chitelet. Work began only in 1975 and is still continuing. With an area of 24 ha it is the largest botanic garden in France and is organised like a museum, so that visitors of any age and any level of expertise can enjoy and learn from it. In this, the founders of the garden have succeeded admirably and it is possible to be engrossed for hours in this extensive garden with its modern glasshouses.

There are five principal collections: the historical collection that displays plants grown from the neolithic age right through to the present together with their dates of introduction. Charlemagne's recommendations for 'plants to be grown in cloisters and towns' is one of the sections

The ornamental collection is based on plants bred by horticulturists from Nancy, an important centre in the first years of this century. Two of the best known are F. F. Crousse, a grower of begonias, peonies and pelargoniums - the ivy-leaved double pink geranium, 'Madame Crousse' and peonies 'Albert Crousse' and 'Felix Crousse', are still widely grown - and Victor Lemoine, who specialised in syringas, fuchsias, philadelphus and deutzias. He was the first foreigner to be awarded a Veitch medal by the Royal Horticultural Society in England.

The alpine collection is on a slope built up with rocks from the Vosges and the plantings are arranged in geographical areas. The neighbouring arboretum-fruticetum is composed of small trees and shrubs. The systematic collection is planned to follow the shape of a genealogical tree, the orders diverging at different levels, going from the most primitive at the top of the site, to the most highly developed plants at the bottom. There is a fascinating homeopathic collection where plants are grouped according to their ability to provide certain minerals used in homeopathy. Plants in danger in their natural habitat are conserved in the ecological sector.

Another interesting planned project is the Jardin d'Emile Gallé. Emile Gallé the artist and glass designer came from Nancy and his creations are known all over the world. He was a keen plantsman and he based his designs on the flowing forms of leaves and flowers. A list has been compiled of all the plants he used in his work and it is intended to make a faithful copy of his garden.

There are eight greenhouses, four open to the public and four reserved for scientific collections. These contain plants collected from their natural habitats including many endangered species, some unidentified. In one of the greenhouses open to the public, the tropical pool house, are a *Victoria amazonica* waterlily and mangroves. The other three houses are for growing useful plants, tropical vegetation and plants from arid areas.

PARC DE LA PEPINIERE
Place de Gaulle, 54000 Nancy

*In the centre of Nancy near the Place Stanislas. (41 D4)* **Opening hours:** *Every day, 6.30am-9pm in winter and 6am-11pm in summer.* **E.** *Free. Wheelchairs. Toilets (and for the handicapped.) Brasserie.*

Stanislas, deposed king of Poland and father-in-law of Louis XV, was responsible for beginning the garden at La Pepinière but Louis himself completed it in 1766. Its eighteenth century character is still visible in the straight avenues of trees that cross the site.

There are some interesting conifers including an *Araucaria aurana,* and a *Sequoiadendron giganteum,* as well as a *Pterocarya fraxinifolia,* and a *Gymnocladus dioica* (Kentucky coffee tree). There is a particularly large and shapely *Clerodendrum trichotomum* with white flowers and turquoise blue berries in late summer.

The mosaiculture or carpet bedding is rather splendid; richly plump and overplanted it reminds one of *fin de siècle* beauties in ostrich plume headdresses. At the far end of the park from the magnificent Place Stanislas is the rose garden, very well kept and in typical French style, with climbing and rambler roses trained on pillars and long chains.

Also in Nancy is the **Parc Ste Marie** in the Avenue du Maréchal-Juin, south of the city centre, near the Cité Judiciaire and the military hospital, with the same opening hours. A natural park with some fine weeping sequoias, cedars and liriodendrons. It has a statue of nurseryman, Victor Lemoine, famous for his work hybridising philadelphus and syringa. Nancy has many other parks, gardens and open spaces including **Parc Olry** with good trees and **Les Jardins du Belvedere**, with fine views over Nancy.

## MOSELLE

### ABBAYE DE GORZE
Centre de soins et d'hébergement, 1 Place du Château, Gorze, 57680 Noveant-sur-Moselle. Tel: 87 52 00 05.

*South west of Metz. Leave the town by N3 to Verdun; at Moulins take left fork on to D6 to Ars-sur-Moselle, Pont-à-Mousson and Nancy. 6 km beyond Ars, at Noveant-sur-Moselle, take the right fork to Gorze along D12. The entrance to the château is in the main square. Go in through archway. (41 D2)* **Opening hours:** *Every day, 9-5. E. Free. Wheelchairs, part is accessible.*

The remains of a classical garden, with fine stonework and *bas-reliefs*, in the grounds of what is now a hospital. The abbey was built at the end of the seventeenth century, in the local yellow chalk. The modest archway on the main square leads to the court of honour which was once paved. The garden is on a higher level than the court and so immediately opposite the entrance is a retaining wall topped by a balustrade and with double access ramps. These ramps are decorated with singularly inappropriate but very fine *bas-reliefs* of the life of Medea. To the right the marriage of Medea to Jason in the presence of the Goddess Aurora, surrc·inded by palm trees and wild flowers is depicted. To the left Medea is carried into the air in a chariot pulled by two dragons. Her murdered children, gouts of blood spurting from their pierced flanks are also shown.

Two *sphynges,* female-breasted sphinxes, survey the access to the *parterre,* now simply grass but possibly to be restored in the future. At the end of the *parterre,* just below the hospital, is a curved cascade with eight niches each containing *hauts-reliefs* of nymphs and water gods, bedecked with palm trees, swans, cherubs, fruit trees, urns and even squirrels climbing trees, all forming fountains from which water flowed into a central pool.

This is a garden for the historian and the architect in a most unlikely setting.

### JARDIN BOTANIQUE, METZ
27 Rue de Pont-à-Mousson, 57158 Montigny-les-Metz.

*South west of city centre, just north of Montigny. (41 D1)* **Opening hours:** *May to September, 7am -9 pm; October to April, 8-6. Greenhouses 9-11.30 and 2-6 (4.45. in winter) E. Free. Toilet. Wheelchairs.*

A municipal park in the *paysager* or landscape style, with some magnificent weeping trees between 100 and 150 years old, including beech, ash, and a

*Sophora japonica,* as well as an *Albizzia julibrissin,* a persimmon, a large collection of bamboos and a good range of conifers.

There are beds of common herbaceous plants, trials of bedding plants, a display of fuchsias and a rose garden with hybrid tea roses and some older shrub roses. The greenhouses contain palms, citrus trees, cacti, coffee and pepper trees.

This is a municipal park rather than a botanic garden - pleasant enough if you are in Metz but not worth a special journey.


## VOSGES

### JARDIN D'ALTITUDE DU HAUT CHITELET
Col de Schlucht, 88400 Gerardmer. Tel: 29 63 31 46.

*West of Colmar on D417 to Gerardmer. Take the Route des Crêtes at Col de Schlucht for 2 km. Haut Chitelet is well signed. (60 C4)* **Opening hours:** *15 May to 31 August, 10-6. From 1 September to 15 October, 10-5.30. E. Inexpensive.*

This twenty year old alpine garden is 4,000 ft high in the Vosges mountains and it contains plants from all the mountainous areas of France, the Vosges, the Jura, the Pyrenees, and Haut Savoie, arranged not in order beds but geographically, as an apparently natural alpine garden. It is at its best in July and the late opening date reflects the fact that before the end of May, the garden is likely to be under snow.

The centre of the garden is devoted to flowers from the Vosges and it includes a tiny bed of native flowers that grow <u>on</u> the châteaux there and in Alsace: sempervivums, saxifrages, sedums and eranthis. Surrounding beds contain collections from mountainous areas of Japan, America, Australia, China, Siberia and the Himalaya.

The river Volognes has its source in the garden and the little rivulet has been formed into pools providing habitats for aquatics and poolside plants. Some of the tiny tributaries seep into the adjoining peat bog which has been conserved in its natural state and is surrounded by beech forest.

There are numbers of different pulsatillas and gentians, from the spring flowering *Gentiana clusii* to the autumn flowering *Swertia aucheri,* from the same family but with white borage-like flowers. From the shrubby *Lonicera alpigena,* native to the Alps and the small leaved *Nothofagus antarctica* from Chile, the plants come from all over the world. There are 3,250 species being cultivated, not including varieties.

## NORD-PAS-DE-CALAIS

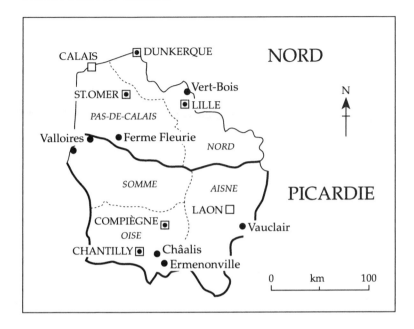

**NORD**

JARDIN DE SCULPTURES DE DUNKERQUE
Avenue des Bains, 59140 Dunkerque. Tel: 28 59 21 65.

*The garden of the Musée d'Art Contemporain is well signed, to the north of the town centre. Take the main road past the Cathedral and turn left at Place Victoire, down the Avenue des Bains. (3 D1)* **Opening hours:** *Every day 10-7.* **E.** *Free. Toilets. Wheelchairs.*

The garden was created in 1979 and includes 18 contemporary sculptures. Curved and sloping paths of interlocking bricks swing round rocky outcrops, making small sheltered spaces to display sculpture or create seating areas. Rusting iron is used as a fence and bold plantings of salt-resistant shrubs and grasses make a very interesting modern garden.

Elaeagnus, sea buckthorn, white poplars and coarse, glaucous grasses, contorted willow and atriplex add their distinctive shapes and cool grey coloring to this site whipped by North Sea winds. Boulders are used like pieces of sculpture. Many ideas here for anyone with a new garden on an exposed site, as well as for landscape architects and those thinking about placing some modern sculpture in a garden.

La Ferme Fleurie is a nursery situated in the 'most flowery village in France' and the main building is lavishly decorated with hanging baskets and containers. The nursery has some 5,000 varieties of plants, arranged as a garden to make a visit interesting all year round. It specialises in gold and silver-leaved plants and has a good herbaceous collection.

JARDIN PUBLIC, ST OMER
Boulevard Vauban, 62500 St Omer.

*In the centre of St Omer.* **Opening hours:** *All year round.* **E.** *Free.*

Well kept public park in the ramparts with some good trees and lawns classically ornamented with cones and domes of clipped box.


**BASSE NORMANDIE**

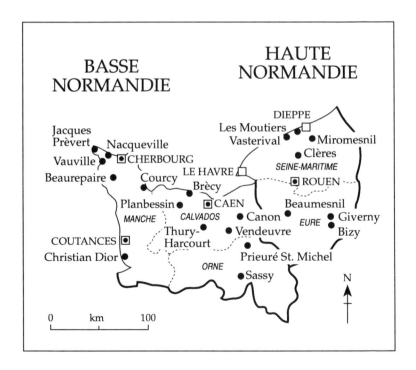

## CALVADOS

CHATEAU DE BRECY
14480 St Gabriel Brécy. Tel: 31 80 11 48.

*Take the N13 from Caen to Bayeux. After about 15 km turn north on the D82 to Martragny, Rucqueville and St Gabriel-Brécy. Turn left after Rucqueville. (13 F4). Opening hours: Easter Sunday to the end of October, Tuesday, Thursday and Sunday 2.30-6.30. E. Inexpensive.*

A narrow lane through the pastoral farming country of Calvados passes a monumental seventeenth century gateway set in a pilastered wall and elaborately decorated with lions, garlands of fruit and flowers. Inside the gate is a simple, bare yard and the château itself is like a plain manor house. However, stepping through a door in the corner of the yard reveals a garden of amazing sophistication and architectural expertise.

The garden is quite small and rises away from the house in five terraces of unequal size, each one different and all designed to give the illusion of a long perspective that continues through a pair of wrought iron gates on the skyline to the green fields beyond. The first terrace is an elaborate *parterre en broderie* in clipped box while the others are simpler with central pools or cones of clipped evergreens.

The stonework - steps, statues, urns, retaining walls decorated with pilasters that echo those of the main gate and rows of stone fruit baskets - is richly exuberant and encrusted with lichen. One of the terraces has a pavilion at each end, another is guarded by two-headed lions of a faintly comical aspect. The thirteenth century parish church is also part of the site.

JARDIN DES PLANTES, CAEN
5 Place Blot, 14000 Caen.

*The château in the centre of Caen is easy to find with a one-way road round a large island on which it sits together with the Museum of Fine Arts and the Museum of Normandy. At the north west corner of the encircling road is the Rue Bosnières with an entrance to the Jardin des Plantes. (32 A1) Opening hours: Every day, 8-sunset. Glasshouses open 2-5. E. Free. Wheelchairs. Toilets.*

This is a particularly attractive public park with a diverse and well-labelled botanic section. The garden was founded in 1736 on its present site and the park area was added as early as 1805, accounting for its well-established appearance. The greenhouses and orangery were built in the 1860s.

In the botanic section there are plant order beds which include the wild flowers and grasses of Normandy. In the spring tulips are well represented, and include such cultivars as black parrot tulips and 'Burgundy Lace'.

Other sections contain trees and shrubs suitable for gardens and utilitarian plants. Beyond this is a rock garden. A well laid out garden of medicinal plants contains beds of aromatic plants and oil and dye producing plants as well as the more common medicinal herbs. Surrounding the order beds is an interesting border of shrubs: *Zanthoxylum planispinum*, choisya, berberis, *Buxus balearica*, *Styrax officinalis* and many others.

The park area is surrounded by large trees underplanted with shrubs: *Diervilla sessilifolia* and *Aronia* x *prunifolia* beneath a huge *Tilia platyphyllos*, Austrian black pines and *Ostrya virginiana* (Ironwood). Other attractive trees include sugar maples, a cut leaved beech and the palm tree *Trachycarpus fortunei*. Plant lovers will find the garden very rewarding.

Also in Caen, **La Vallée des Jardins** by the Boulevard Weygand with a collection of peonies and day lilies and a **Jardin des Simples** within the Castle walls.

Canon

CHATEAU DE CANON
14270 Mézidon. Tel: 31 20 02 72.

*Midway between Caen and Lisieux. Turn south off the N13 between Lion d'Or and Croissanville, on to the D152 to Mézidon. Canon is on the edge of Mézidon on the Caen side. (32 B2)* **Opening hours:** *Easter to 30 June, Saturday, Sunday and holidays 2-7. 1 July to 30 September, every afternoon except Tuesday 2-7. E.Very moderate. Wheelchairs. Toilets.*

The garden at the château of Canon has remained unchanged since the mid-eighteenth century when it was created by Elie de Beaumont between 1768 and 1783. It is full of romantic notions and eccentricities and is particularly interesting for its combination of French and English picturesque styles and for its Anglo-Chinese garden. This mixture of styles, plus the devotion and skill of the owners, M. and Mme Mézerac, make Canon a delightful garden to visit.

Through the gates at the end of the long avenue the symmetrical façade of the château can be seen across the *cour d'honneur*, where, instead of standing on a velvet *tapis vert*, (lawn), statues are dotted among waving grass which in spring is scattered with fringed yellow doronicums.

Continuing along the main axis, the back façade of the château is reflected in a large rectangular *miroir d'eau*, its surface broken with waterlilies and an inquisitive swan. At the end, a semi-circle of Carrara marble busts of *commedia dell'arte* characters from the popular comedies of sixteenth century Italy, gaze towards the house.

The major transverse axis runs from a lacquer-red Chinese pavilion that was rescued from the Château des Ternes in Paris, and from where it is possible to see the fields beyond, to the white memorial temple to Elie de Beaumont's wife, which was erected in 1783. Between these two follies, a circular pigeon loft which would have stuck out into the path, has been sliced in half and the remainder refaced to give a classical appearance. In the tiny wood with its streams of clear water, the ruined Château de Berenger is preserved as a romantic feature. In this same area, a lawyer friend of M de Beaumont designed the Anglo-Chinese garden, planted with Oriental plane trees and clumps of evergreens around a small lake.

The prettiest part of the garden is the Chartreuses, a series of interlinked walled enclosures designed originally for growing fruit trees. Today a statue of Pomona looks through a series of diminishing arches between the enclosures that give a false perspective. Each of the enclosures is an exuberantly planted flower garden, at its best in July and August.

## PARC ET JARDINS DU CHATEAU D'HARCOURT
14220 Thury-Harcourt. Tel: 31 79 65 41.

*26 km south of Caen on D562 in the direction of Laval. The château ruins are on the south side of Thury-Harcourt on the west side of the road. The gardens are behind the ruined château. (32 A2)* **Opening Hours:** *April and October, Sundays and holidays, 2.30-6.30; May to September every day, 2.30-6.30. E. Moderate. Wheelchairs. Toilets.*

The entrance to the garden is by the dramatic remains of the Château d'Harcourt. The path goes between a wood and the edge of a meadow planted with narcissi and daffodils, then alongside a decorative hedge with cherry trees, viburnum and forsythia and new plantings of lilac, philadelphus and other flowering shrubs. A long tunnel of trees creates a tempting path that simply has to be explored, and which leads to the pastoral valley of the River Orne.

The summer garden is in the opposite direction, on a lower level and enclosed by trees. It is a garden mainly of annual flowers, designed to be at its best in high summer when the garden is open every day. A large lawn is divided into four by paths that cross in the centre. The paths are bordered on both sides by narrow beds predominantly of annuals in delicate, light colors. The effect from above is of a lawn laid with strips of multi-colored voile, very pretty, but slightly flimsy. Roses and hibiscus are permanent occupants of the beds and the annuals vary each year. Cleomes, coreopsis, cosmos, phlox and delphiniums give height to antirrhinums, *Salvia farinacea*, zinnias, ageratum and verbena. The plants are placed carefully to ensure a harmonious effect. This garden is linked to the Pavillon de Fantaisie, once an orangery and dairy for the château, by a rose garden and a triangular herbaceous bed planted with rock roses, catmint, dianthus, cornflowers and campanulas, spiked with irises, day lilies and *Allium albopilosum*.

## PLANBESSIN
14490 Castillon. Tel: 31 92 56 03.

*Take the D572 from Bayeux to St Lô and at La Tuilerie/Noron le Poterie, take the turning to Castillon, the D73. (13 E3)* **Opening hours:** *Monday to Friday 2-5. Saturday 2-5 by appointment. E. Inexpensive.*

A delightful garden with beautifully grown plants, attached to a specialist herbaceous plant nursery. There is a pergola with climbing plants, a herb garden, a herbaceous border and rectangular and hexagonal pools.

There are good collections of hardy geraniums and hydrangeas, foliage plants and herbs, together with some fine trees, including magnolias, *Acer griseum, Prunus serrula* and *Betulus nigra*.

While in the area, don't miss the sight of the splendidly situated **Château de Balleroy** at the end of the main street in Balleroy. There is a small but very fine *parterre* in front.

## CHATEAU DE VENDEUVRE
14170 St-Pierre-sur-Dives. Tel: 31 40 93 83.

*30 km south east of Caen. Take the A13 Caen-Lisieux and after 9 km take the D40 to St-Pierre. At St-Pierre, take the D511 to Falaise. Vendeuvre is 4 km. (32 C2)* **Opening hours:** *1 March to 1 May, weekends and holidays 2-6; 1 May to 1 October, every day 2-6; 1 October to 2 November, weekends and holidays, 2-6. **E.** Moderate. Wheelchairs. Toilets. Salon du Thé in July and August.*

The original gardens at Vendeuvre were transformed into a *jardin à l'anglaise* in 1830 and subsequently damaged during World War II. They are currently being restored in the spirit of the original design.

The main axis has a *jardin à la française* in front of the building and a new *miroir d'eau* behind. The cross axis is a fine avenue of limes dating from the eighteenth century with buildings like the dovecote and an ice-house nearby. A path between two labyrinths of box leads to the water gardens. One section, the Jardins d'Eau Surprise, includes trick fountains and water jokes. The oriental bridge that spurts jets of water as it is trodden on, the Crystal Tree and the Fountain of the Muses are in place. Two new *jeux d'eau* were created for 1994.

Other features include a pyramid, the Temple of Serenity, a belvedere on one of the islands and a new arboretum.


## MANCHE

## DOMAINE DE BEAUREPAIRE, MARTINVAST
50690 Martinvast. Tel: 33 52 02 23. Fax: 33 52 03 01.

*7 km from Cherbourg on the D904 to Barneville Carteret, then the D900 to Martinvast. Signed 'Martinvast' rather than Beaurepaire. (12 B2)* **Opening hours:** *August, every day, 2-7;1 April to 1 November, weekends and holidays, 2-7; 4 November to 26 March, weekends and holidays, 2-6. **E.** Moderate. Toilets.*

The park at Beaurepaire was created in the English style in 1820. There are very extensive lakes, streams, waterfalls and an eighteenth century obelisk at the end of a perspective. Rhododendrons and tulip trees grow well in this wooded park as do some fine conifers. There is a section of garden with rare rhododendron species of enormous size.

## JARDIN CHRISTIAN DIOR
Rue d'Estouteville, 50400 Granville.

*Off the Avenue de la Liberation, on the D971 to Coutances, north of the Haute Ville.* **Opening hours:** *Every day, 8-sunset. E. Free Wheelchairs, part is accessible.*

A walled garden with both sheltered corners and sea views, surrounding a blancmange pink villa. In front of the house the master's 'New Look' is rendered in mosaiculture. A rose walk, a rectangular paddling pool, a pergola with a plum tree trained over it and a portrait bust of Dior set on a bleak granite pillar are also to be found.

## CHATEAU DE COURCY
Fontenay-sur-Mer, 50310 Montebourg. Tel: 33 41 14 56.

*12 km east of Valognes.* **Opening hours:** *Tuesday to Saturday from Easter to All Saints, 2-5 . E. Free.*

Well kept lawns, a formal *parterre à la française* surrounded by a moat with swans, a lake, dovecote and an old *potager* which has been made into a rose garden are features of this château garden.

## JARDIN PUBLIC, COUTANCES
Rue Quesnel Canveaux, 50200 Coutances.

*Near the cathedral square where it is possible to park.* **Opening hours:** *Every day from 9-5 in winter, 9-8 in spring and autumn, 11pm in summer. E. Free. Toilets*

This is a pleasant municipal park on a steeply sloping site, with amazing bedding. There is a rose walk, each rose having its own little overhead lamp. On the credit side, there are Italianate terraces, an interesting mound, circled by hedges of clipped hornbeam which makes a small labyrinth and some impressive trees, Cedar of Lebanon, *Gymnocladus dioica, Nothofagus antarctica* and an *Aesculus flava* (yellow buckeye).

## JARDINS JACQUES PREVERT
50440 St-Germain-des-Vaux.

*28 km west of Cherbourg on the D901 or D45 towards Cap de la Hague, then take path facing the Port Racine Route Touristique.* **Opening hours:** *May-September, every day except Wednesday, 2-7. Open Wednesdays July-August. E. Moderate.*

This garden of 1 ha, traversed by a small stream complete with red-trimmed footbridges, was created as an act of homage to the poet Jacques Prévert who was a close friend of the owner. It is a very original setting for plants given in memory of the poet by friends and admirers.

## CHATEAU DE NACQUEVILLE
50460 Urville-Nacqueville. Tel: 33 03 56 03.

*6 km west of Cherbourg on the north coastal road. Take the D45 from Cherbourg to Querqueville and Urville-Nacqueville. At the hamlet of La Rivière, take the first left turn. Parking by the gatehouse. There is quite a long walk to the château. (12 A1)* **Opening hours:** *Easter to 30 September, every day except Tuesdays and Fridays which are not holidays. Guided visits only, at 2, 3, 4 and 5 pm. E. Very moderate.*

It is difficult to believe that this English style park was destroyed in the last war by the Germans who felled the trees to make posts for the Atlantic wall and then by the Americans who built barracks. Now it is a tranquil green valley sheltered by wooded escarpments and with a small stream, thickly bordered with arum lilies, that falls into a long lake planted round with rhododendrons, azaleas and dramatic giant *Gunnera manicata*. Palm trees create an exotic effect, framing a view of the sea, while hydrangeas flourish here, too. A delightful ivy-covered gatehouse, with round towers and conical roofs, adds a fairy-tale element to the English park. It is at its best at the end of May when the rhododendrons are in flower. The guided tour of 55 minutes does not allow much time to enjoy the garden.


## VAUVILLE
50440 Beaumont-Hague.

*West of Cherbourg on D901 to Beaumont and Cap de la Hague. Old Norman Castle next to the church.* **Opening hours:** *May to 30 September, Sundays and Tuesdays, 2-6. E. Guided tours. Moderate. Wheelchairs, part is accessible. Toilets.*

Madame Pellerin's fascinating garden was featured in 'The Private Gardens of France' but was severely hit by three bad winters and the hurricane of 1987. Now the exotic and tender plants that are such a feature of the garden are flourishing again.

The garden layout is very informal, with broad grass paths and grassy pockets around which are planted exotic and succulent plants more often seen in the south of France. Agaves, aloes and forests of echiums are planted in broad bands throughout the garden and they remain outside all year. The garden was started in 1947 and the plants survived normal winters in their maritime situation until the extreme conditions of the mid-1980s. Subsequent mild winters have enabled the garden to return to its former richness. The yuccas, agapanthus, and tritonias are accompanied by bamboos, by brooms and cistus from Corsica, and by irises, crinums and gunnera in the damper areas.

All the plants were initially gifts or exchanges and many are now propagated at Vauville. There is a wide range of plants in an attractive setting reminiscent of a Cornish valley garden.

## ORNE

PRIEURE SAINT-MICHEL
Crouttes, 61120 Vimoutiers. Tel: 33 39 15 15.

*Vimoutiers is 30 km from Lisieux. In Vimoutiers, take the D916 to Argentan and after 4 km. take the turning to Crouttes. **Opening hours:** Weekends and holidays from Pentecost to 18 September; 12 July to 15 August, every day 2-7. E. Moderate. Wheelchairs. Toilets.*

The gardens of the thirteenth century Benedictine priory have been partly designed by landscape architect Louis Benech and horticulturalists G.Delbard. There are rose, iris and water gardens, a garden of grasses and a monastic style *potager* containing old varieties of vegetables, aromatic and medicinal plants. The gardens are sited around some fine monastic buildings, including a fifteenth century cider press and thirteenth century tithe barn, now used for cultural events.

CHATEAU DE SASSY
61570 Mortrée. Tel: 33 35 32 66.

*South of Argentan on the N158 to Alençon. After 9.5 km turn right into St Christophe-le-Jajolet, go through the village and then turn left. (32 C4) **Opening hours:** From Palm Sunday to All Saints, every day from 3-6. In the morning, on demand. E. Moderate.*

The lovely château in soft pink brick and stone, stands on a hill overlooking the valley of the river Baize, a tributary of the Orne. It is beautifully sited, looking over three descending terraces to a formal garden with elaborate arabesques of clipped box.

Both the gardens and the château have an eighteenth century formality which by its ordered perfection, quite takes the breath away. This is particularly surprising as the château was begun in 1760, not finished when the Revolution broke out, and was only completed under the Restoration. The long wing that separates the *cour d'honneur* from the stables, dates from the beginning of this century.

# HAUTE NORMANDIE

## EURE

### CHATEAU DE BEAUMESNIL
27410 Beaumesnil. Tel: 32 44 40 09.

*13 km south east of Bernay on the D140 to Conches. (33 F2)* **Opening hours:** *Château, Easter to 30 September, Friday, Saturday, Sunday , Monday and holidays; July and August, every day, 2.30-6. Gardens: 1 May to 15 October every day except Tuesday. E. Château, moderate; Gardens, inexpensive. Wheelchairs. Toilets.*

La Quintinye the great horticulturist who worked with Le Nôtre at Versailles was the designer of these gardens, unchanged since they were created in about 1640. The highly decorated brick and stone château is said to be the finest Louis XIII château in existence and a very early example of French baroque architecture. It is surrounded by impressive moats in which three sides of the château are mirrored. The west façade overlooks an imposing *cour d'honneur* bordered with hedges of clipped yew. There are several separate sections of formal garden: the main ones are the Demi-Lune and the Garden of Madame. The half moon shaped garden is on the other side of the moat from the château. It has a curved *parterre* and is decorated with box balls, statues and urns. The most unusual feature is the labyrinth on a circular mound over the foundations of a mediaeval donjon.

A wisteria covered archway separates sections of the garden and there is a pleasant walk round the lake behind. In the park, the *allées* of the seventeenth and eighteenth century still remain. It is very well maintained.

### CHATEAU DE BIZY
27200 Vernon. Tel: 35 51 00 82.

*3 km from Giverny. Take the D181 out of Vernon signed to Pacy-sur-Eure and Evreux. The château is oon the edge of the town, at the end of a magnificent avenue of clipped limes. (34 C2)* **Opening hours:** *Every day except Monday from 1 April to 1 November, 10-12 and 2-6. 2 November to 31 March, weekends, 2-5. E. Guided tours, moderate. Wheelchairs. Toilets.*

A château garden in the grand manner. The *cour d'honneur* is enclosed by the original eighteenth century stables and with a central fountain and clipped box, is very satisfying. Most of the château is a nineteenth century reconstruction with a pillared façade in the style of Louis XVI. Only a small part of the park with its baroque statues can be visited. The cascades and statuary behind the house are particularly interesting. The central axis was restored in 1994 and although there is water in the fountains more work has to be done before they return to their full glory.

## MUSEE CLAUDE MONET
Musée Claude Monet, 27620 Giverny. Tel: 32 51 28 21.

*The village of Giverny is on the D5, on the other side of the river Seine from the town of Vernon - cross the river and take the first on the right, the D5, to La Roche Guyon. Giverny is 5 km and the Fondation Claude Monet is well signed. Buses leave from Vernon Railway Station at 1.15 and 3.20 and return from Giverny at 12.45 and 5.10 in the season. Taxis from Vernon town centre, five minutes' walk from the station. (34 C2)* **Opening hours:** *Every day except Monday, 1 April to 31 October, 10-6.* **E.** *Moderate for museum and gardens, very moderate for garden alone. Toilets.*

Monet's garden, restored by the Institut de Beaux Arts with the help of generous American donations, was first opened in 1980. It has now developed the luxuriance and lavishness that it had in Monet's day and is very popular. However, Giverny is a garden on a domestic scale and was not designed for crowds. The magical atmosphere is destroyed by too many people and recent visitors have found their visits less than satisfactory. If you absolutely must go, try to go outside July and August and on a week-day morning or perhaps over the lunch period.

This is so obviously the garden of an Impressionist painter. Shimmering color and richly scented flowers seem more intensely sensuous than in any other garden. The Clos Normand, the section of garden in front of the house, is like a cottage garden with straight paths and rectangular beds full of simple flowers: tulips and forget-me-nots, double daisies, violas and wallflowers, Jacob's ladders and primulas. These are followed by peonies, irises, shrub roses, hundreds of lilies, poppies, pinks, nasturtiums and phlox. The plants are grown, densely and with a sure eye for color. The forget-me-nots are pink, the tulips yellow, edged with red or white with pink feathering or a deep violet. The nasturtiums scramble all over the beds and across the wide, central gravel path. Roses and clematis are trained up formal arches and pyramid frames but the rigid shapes are completely lost amid a swirl of flower, leaf and curling tendril.

At the bottom of this garden is a tunnel under the busy D5 to the Japanese water garden, with its wisteria-festooned bridge and the water lilies, so familiar from Claude Monet's paintings.

Monet lived at Giverny from 1883 until 1926, buying the house for its nearness to the little river Epte and for the quality of light in that part of Normandy. A passion for gardening rapidly developed and in the end became as great as his love for painting. He was 'ecstatic about flowers' but also, like all true gardeners, had a sensuous love for the very texture of the earth in which they grew.

Because of his paintings and thousands of photographs - his household was full of keen photographers - it has been possible for the Fondation to recreate the garden in all its variety, faithful to the spirit of the original. Giverny is not only one of the most recorded, but also one of the most written-about gardens in France.

## SEINE MARITIME

### CLERES
76690 Clères. Tel: 35 33 23 08.

*41 km south of Dieppe and 22 km north of Rouen. Turn east from the N27 on to the D6 at le Boulay. Well signposted from shortly outside Dieppe. (16 A2)* **Opening hours:** *Summer, every day 9-6 or 7; spring and autumn, every day 9-12 and 1.30-5 or 6. Last entry, one hour before closure. Closed from 1 December to mid-March. E . Moderate. Toilets. Wheelchairs.*

Clères is owned by the Muséum National d'Histoire Naturelle and it has an educative function rather than a commercial one. Although popular, no attempts are made to commercialise the garden. Even so, avoid peak holiday periods and weekends.

The château dates from the eleventh century and the original building, now a picturesque ruin behind the main château, once sheltered Joan of Arc. The gardens were created in 1920 by Jean Delacour with the help of Avray Tipping.

In front is a low border in which aubrieta, alyssum, iberis, bluebells, cowslips and tulips form a multi-colored and ever changing ribbon. On the walls of the château are *Actinidia kolomitka* and *Actinidia deliciosa* (Chinese gooseberry) together with roses, honeysuckle and wisteria.

A wild flower lawn leads down to the lake and streams where waterfowl, herons, flamingoes and giant gunnera add exotic notes to what is basically a country house garden. A wilder, steeper area where deer, wallabies and gibbons roam free over the grass and peacocks noisily conduct their courtship rituals under a fine group of copper beeches, gives way to the animal enclosures where antelopes, emus and pheasants are kept.

### MIROMESNIL
Tourville-sur-Arques, 76550 Offranville. Tel: 35 04 40 30. Fax: 35 85 02 80.

*Leave Dieppe on the N27 to Rouen. After 6 km, at St Aubin-sur-Scie, take a left turn at the traffic lights to D54, signed to Arques-les-Batailles. Turn on to the D254 and the château is signed.* **Opening hours:** *1 May to 15 October, 2-6, closed on Tuesdays. Guided tours of château and garden. E . Moderate. Wheelchairs. Toilets.*

The château is set in the middle of acres of woodland, and reached by imposing avenues of beech trees and the lawn is surrounded by more fine trees. Guy de Maupassant was born there. The main feature of interest for the gardener is the *potager* or walled kitchen garden, still cultivated in the traditional way with a mixture of vegetables, fruit and flowers. Gnarled fruit trees with a group of luxuriant peonies grow alongside immaculate rows of carrots, French beans and artichokes. Walks are lined with daffodils, roses, delphiniums and dahlias succeeding each other through the season, while the walls support a good collection of clematis.

PARC FLORAL DES MOUTIERS
Route de l'Eglise, 79119 Varengeville-sur-Mer. Tel: 35 85 10 02.

*West of Dieppe on the D75 to St Valery and Varengeville. Well signed.(16 A1).*
**Opening hours:** *Every day mid-March to mid-November, 10-12 and 2-6. E Moderate. Wheelchairs. Toilets.*

In 1898, when Edwin Lutyens was a young man, he was commissioned by his friend Guillaume Mallet to build a house on the edge of a valley running down to the Normandy cliffs. Le Bois de Moutiers is the only Arts and Crafts house in France. Lutyens also designed the garden and the style and detailing which were to become associated with him can be seen in the long, rose-covered pergola with brick pillars which ends in a Chinese pavilion, the brick paths, the tile-capped walls that divide the sections of the garden, and the curved stone and tile seats. The art of Gertrude Jekyll, Lutyens' great collaborator in so many English gardens, can be sensed. She sent drawings for mixed borders and gave advice for the planting in the woodland park.

Another spirit in the garden is that of Vita Sackville-West. This can be felt especially in the white garden where very formal box-edged beds contain a lavish planting of white flowers in a profusion and variety not often seen in France. The main planting is of 'White Triumphator' tulips in the spring, followed by 'Iceberg roses', with many other covetable white flowered plants tucked in and around them: *Caltha palustris* 'alba', *Astrantia major* 'Sunningdale variegata', white forms of liatris, pulmonaria and dicentra and, against the walls, *Rhodotypos scandens, Eremurus aitchisonii, Hydrangea anomala petiolaris* and *Salvia sclarea alba*.

The magnolia orchard is at its best in April while the two large mixed borders, given substance with rugosa roses, *Buddleja alternifolia* and *Kolkwitzia amabilis*, are lovely in spring with lemon-cream colored daffodils, peach-colored tulips and deep purple pulmonaria, and in summer with herbaceous plants. Beyond the magnolia orchard a new rose garden has been laid out. Mature bushes and rambler roses hint at the enjoyment to come.

Les Moutiers

The woodland garden, with its vistas inspired originally by drawings of Claude Lorrain, is by far the largest part of the park. Beneath such trees as liquidambars, hollies, pines, red oaks and blue cedars, grow rhododendrons and azaleas, magnolias, exochorda and viburnum. Beneath them, *allium ursinum*, bluebells, anemones, lady smock, violets, primroses and Solomon's seal are to be found. In the valley a boggy area with rheums and peltiphyllum, is created by natural springs.

This garden is ideally situated as a first or last port of call for anyone travelling on the Dieppe ferry.

## JARDIN DES PLANTES, ROUEN
114 avenue des Martyrs-de-la-Résistance, 76100 Rouen.

*South of the town centre, go towards Les Essarts interchange of the A13 to Caen and Evreux. At Rond Point des Bruyères, before the broad Avenue des Canadiens, go round three-quarters of the roundabout and back up the Avenue of the Martyrs of the Résistance. The entrance to the Jardin des Plantes is on the left. Parking near the bus stop. Bus: Line no. 12, Jardin des Plantes. (16 A4)* **Opening hours:** *Every day 8-5.30 in winter and 8-8 in summer. E .Free. Wheelchairs (Part of greenhouses only are accessible). Special Braille plan for the blind. Toilets (basic).*

A public park with many interesting plants. Near the entrance there is a specimen of the unusual twisted beech, the Faux de Verzy. In the distance, lines of flowering crabs and brilliant bedding lead up to an attractive greenhouse which was built in 1839, shortly after the Jardin des Plantes was formally opened on this site. Now the greenhouses have collections of succulent plants and useful plants like coffee, pepper and banana trees. The tropical house has a tank with a fine *Victoria amazonica* water lily while a more temperate house holds the Eugene Boulet collection of orchids and bromeliads.

The order beds contain native plants like *Allium ursinum* and *Cydonia oblonga* as well as collections of sempervivums and some sedums. A narrow canal nearby is edged with *Iris ensata (kaempferi)* and *Iris pseudacorus bastardii.*

A large rock bank has clematis used as a ground cover, scrambling amidst clumps of *Veronica pectinata* 'Rosea', with magenta pink petals edged in white and *Viola hispida*, the Rouen Pansy.

## LE VASTERIVAL
76119 Sainte-Marguerite-sur-Mer. Tel: 35 85 12 05.

*West of Dieppe and Varengeville sur Mer. Take the turning to Phare d'Ailly. The house is unmarked and visits are only by appointment. Although this book is restricted to gardens that are open to the public without prior arrangement, no gardener, botanist or plantsman should miss this garden. It is possible to write beforehand, or telephone and arrange to join one of the many groups that are taken round every day. E Very expensive. Wheelchairs, part is accessible.*

Vasterival is a woodland garden, on a hilly site, full of winding paths and informal shapes. It was started in 1957 and the purpose of the garden is to grow plants well and show them to their best advantage. This means careful placing of each plant so that it is growing in the best possible place for it and next to other plants that, by contrast of form, texture of foliage and color, enhance its appearance.

In practice this means that even quite large plants are moved two or three times until exactly the right site is found. There are traditional borders in the flat area near the house but most of the borders are mixed: there are trees, shrubs, ground cover including herbaceous plants and bulbs - a four tier system that ensures interest at all seasons of the year. The garden is particularly interesting in winter.

Grassy glades are surrounded by beds of heathers, native plants like astrantia, geraniums and narcissi. Banks of species rhododendrons clothe the sides of the valley that wanders down towards sea level, following the course of a stream made by the owner and beautifully planted with *Iris ensata (kaempferi)*, gunnera, astilbes, primulas and *Petasites fragrans* .

It is quite impossible to give a list of plants in the garden, even of rarities: the garden contains over 15,000 different species. It is only possible to give an indication of the scope of one or two different areas. The gold border is planted with heathers, robinia and golden elder, together with *Fagus sylvaticus pendula aurea* (golden-leaved beech) and a variegated hypericum, *H. androsaemum* 'Gladys Brabazon' while *Pinus parviflora* (Japanese white pine) is a noteworthy occupant of the silver border. A border of blue and mauve contains *Cotinus coggygria* partnered by *Erysimum* 'Bowles Mauve'. The orange and red border pairs lonicera and orange fruited crab apples. A *Cornus controversa* 'Variegata' is contrasted with an underplanting of ferns and *Clematis* 'Niobe' grows into a *Pyrus salicifolia*. 'Pendula'. New plantings include a collection of oaks and many new hydrangea cultivars which love the rich, acid clay soil. Two exciting rarities are a *Ginkgo biloba* 'Horizontalis' and a *Pterostyrax corymbosa*.

## PICARDIE
Map: see page 29

### AISNE

ABBAYE DE VAUCLAIR
02860 Bouconville-Vauclair

*30 km north west of Reims. Take the N44 to Laon, turn left at Corbeny on to D62, and after 7 km left again. From Soissons take the N2 to Laon. After 15 km turn right on to the Chemin des Dames. Just after the Caverne du Dragon and before the farm of Hurtebise, turn to the left. The Abbey is well signed. (19 F3) **Opening hours:** Every day 8-8. E Free. Wheelchairs. Toilets in the exhibition hall.*

A garden of medicinal plants behind the ruins of the Cistercian abbey founded by St Bernard in 1134.

In a peaceful setting by the monks' pond, the herbs are set out in a chequerboard of alternate slabs and planting areas. Shrubs like the Provins rose, the cut-leaved *Sambucus nigra* 'laciniata' and a splendid white *Phytolacca americana* (giant pokeweed) shelter the area on one side. The plants are well labelled in French and Latin, the name of the family given and those that are poisonous are marked with a red spot. There is a large information centre which describes the uses of 400 different species of medicinal plant.

## OISE

### ABBAYE DE CHAALIS
60305 Fontaine-Chaâlis. Tel: 44 54 04 02. Fax: 44 54 07 90.

*Take the N324 Crépy-en-Valois road out of Senlis and turn on to the N330 to Ermenonville and Meaux. The abbey ruins are well signed and are on the left opposite the tourist attraction of La Mer de Sable just north of Ermenonville. (36 B2) **Opening hours:** Park open all year, every day except Tuesday, 9-7. E. Park only, inexpensive. Toilets. Wheelchairs.*

The Abbaye de Chaâlis estate contains the Abbey ruins and the Musée Jacquemart-André, as well as the park and rose garden.

In front of the building in which the museum is housed there is a formal *parterre* ending in a long canal bordered by limes, a focal statue and a view over the surrounding woods and farmland. Near the house, the grass *parterre* is decorated with unclipped cones of yew, statues and urns. Three pools separate the two areas.

On the way to the rose garden do not miss the chapel. It has a fine painted domed ceiling. The walled rose garden is planted with the rose 'Clair Matin' and hybrid tea roses are grown in the central box edged beds. Worth a visit if you are in the area visiting Chantilly or Ermenonville.

### CHATEAU AND MUSEE CONDE, CHANTILLY
60631 Chantilly. Tel: 44 57 08 00. Fax: 44 57 70 31.

*North of Paris and west of Senlis. Well signed and unmissable. (36 A1) **Opening hours:** Park, every day 10-6. E. Moderate. Toilets (in the Hameau) Wheelchairs.*

With the two châteaux (the Musée Condé and the Château d'Enghien), the Grandes Ecuries (great stables) and the Jeu de Paume (the covered tennis court that is now a museum), the centre of Chantilly is very magnificent. There is a great feeling of space as well as grandeur and, indeed, there needs to be for the town is extremely busy with tourists, coach loads of schoolchildren, racegoers and horseboxes. Fireworks and a tethered hot-air balloon in the park add to the hurly-burly in the summer.

The Musée Condé is housed in the Grand Château, rebuilt in about 1880, the original building of Louis XIV's great general, Le Grand Condé, having been destroyed in the Revolution. The château was originally built on its watery site to give it some natural defences. By the seventeenth century the need for châteaux to be defended had disappeared and André le Nôtre, who believed his design for the Prince of Condé at Chantilly to be among his greatest works, was able to transform the defensive moats into watery *parterres*. He increased the area of water by building a Grand Canal on a cross axis to the main *parterre*, using the waters of the river Nonette first to fill a circular pool, then to cascade down into an hexagonal pool and then to form the canal. There is a splendid view from the captive balloon.

The great terrace with its equestrian statue of Anne de Montmorency, the first inhabitant of the château, is the focal point of the T-shaped canal. The château itself is to one side and is surrounded by a sheet of water. The dramatic statues of river gods concealed beneath the terrace can only be seen when looking back from the *parterre*.

On the left is the *jardin anglais* with its winding paths and lakes and the temple of Venus while to the right is a smaller canal and the *hameau*, little brown and white cottages round a tiny lawn with annual flowers and a working water wheel.

The Maison de Sylvie which, like the *hameau* and the Petit Château or Capitanerie (joined to the Grand Chateau), escaped the depredations of the Revolution, has also been restored. It was built in 1604 and was once home to poet Théophile de Viau. It is to the right of the entrance to the gardens through the Grille d'Honneur with its two pretty pavilions.

COMPIEGNE
60200 Compiègne. Tel: 44 38 47 00. Fax: 44 38 47 01.

*The town is 82 km north of Paris. The huge château is easy to find, situated where the town meets the forest of Compiègne, and well signed. The best entrance is in the Place du General de Gaulle, where there is plenty of parking space. (18 B4)*
**Opening hours:** *Gardens, every day 8-sunset. E. Free. Wheelchairs. Toilets.*

The Petit Parc is the name given to the garden that surrounds the château; the Grand Parc is the surrounding forest, reputed to be the finest beech forest in France. The garden was started under Louis XV by J.-A. Gabriel but the Grande Allèe des Beaux Monts, the splendid vista that is seen at its best from the terrace, was continued by L.M. Berthault under Napoleon I. The avenue extends to the horizon and the lions and classical figures that ornament the balustrade of the terrace make an appropriate foreground to the imposing prospect.

Below the terrace, a large trellis covered walk or *berceau* planted with wisteria, climbing hydrangea, aristolochia and campsis, cuts through two large shrub borders. Plant introductions of the 2nd Empire are used. It is suggested that this walk was designed 'for the pleasure of the homesick Empress Marie-Louise, in imitation of her favourite promenade at Schönbrunn'. Near Place General du Gaulle there is a small classical garden with symmetrical temples surrounded by pleached limes.

PARC JEAN-JACQUES ROUSSEAU
60950 Ermenonville.

*South east of Senlis on the N330 to Meaux. (36 B2)* **Opening hours:** *Entry from the village , every day except Tuesday, 2-6.15. E .Inexpensive. Wheelchairs.*

The park at Ermenonville was designed by the Marquis de Girardin, Jean Jacques Rousseau's last patron, as an ideal landscape, one in which beauty and use went hand in hand. The embellishment of the countryside was combined with improved farming methods to produce happy peasants and healthy animals. Girardin believed in Rousseau's ideas about the inherent goodness of nature and the rural life and he was also influenced by the English poet William Shenstone who created the first *ferme ornée* at The Leasowes in Warwickshire in the middle of the eighteenth century.

Ermenonville embodied a completely new concept of garden and landscape and is one of the most important historic gardens in France; the site has been restored to a worthwhile state only in recent years.

Columns, benches and ruins are introduced into a natural park of grass, trees and water, designed to create particular emotions in visitors as they follow the path around the lake. A prehistoric dolmen reminds us of our origins. The deliberately unfinished Temple de la Philosophie is carved with the names of philosophers. The grotto of the Naiads creates the feeling of a descent into the underworld.

La Rêverie, the Table des Mères and several other artefacts including the Banc de la Reine, which was named after Marie Antoinette who is reputed to have cut off her hair in homage to Rousseau at this spot,survive. Rousseau's tomb, though without his remains which were taken to the Pantheon during the Revolution, is still visible on the Ile des Peupliers.

A busy road and an adjoining campsite detract from the park's tranquillity but it is still a fine place for a meditative stroll.

## SOMME

### BAGATELLE, ABBEVILLE
133 route de Paris, 80100 Abbeville. Tel: 42 56 19 84.

*Well signed in the town. Follow the signs to Paris and Beauvais from the centre and just past the Church of St Gilles, take the left fork along the Route de Paris. Bagatelle is on the left. (6 C3)* **Opening hours:** *Every day except Tuesday.1st weekend in July to 1st weekend in September, from 2-6 E .Inexpensive, for château, Museum de France 1940 and the Parc Botanique.*

The small symmetrical garden with lime walks, a grass *parterre* and two statues of cherubs, is surrounded by a park with a good variety of trees including a horseshoe of lime trees.

At the time of visiting the garden was neglected. The château itself is extremely pretty, of rose pink brick and very delicately decorated and there are pictures and paintings inside of how the garden used to be. Now, unfortunately, it is disappointing.

### JARDIN DE VALLOIRES
Abbaye de Valloires, 80120 Argoules. Tel: 22 23 53 55.

*90 km south of Calais and 30 km north of Abbeville. Take the D12 at Nampont or D175 at Vron, east off the N1 to Argoules and Valloires.(6 C2).* **Opening hours:** *18 February to 12 November, evey day, 10-5 ; 10-7 from May to September. E. Moderate, varies according to season.Wheelchairs. Toilets (and for the handicapped) Salon de Thé. Plant centre supplied by Blooms of Bressingham.*

The new gardens of the eighteenth century Abbey at Valloires have been designed to contain the 3,000 plant species and varieties collected by Jean-Louis Cousin, a nurseryman of Saint Georges. The major part of the collection consists of flowering shrubs, many from the north of China where the climate is similar to that of Picardy.

The shrubs are planted in island beds with different themes where they can be seen well, and they are all properly labelled. An avenue of flowering cherries divides this informal planting from the more formal parts of the garden where the design has echoes of the original Cistercian abbey. As well as an attractively planted cloister, there is a white garden, a rose garden and a bog garden. The rose garden, contains many old roses but also new English roses chosen to harmonise with the softer tones of the old roses, and for their scent. In the bog garden, a long canal is bordered by irises, silver birches and dogwoods.This garden, opened for the first time in April 1989, looks set to become an essential detour for gardeners arriving or leaving France via Calais, Boulogne and Dieppe.

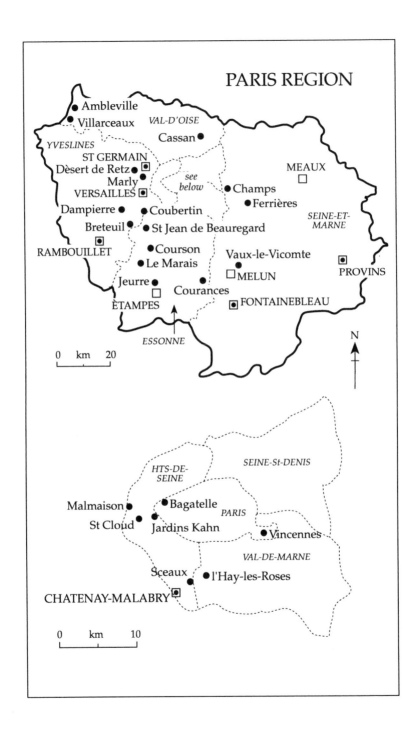

PARIS REGION

Ambleville
Villarceaux
YVESLINES
VAL-D'OISE
Cassan
ST GERMAIN
Dèsert de Retz
MEAUX
Marly
see below
VERSAILLES
Champs
Ferrières
Dampierre
Coubertin
SEINE-ET-MARNE
Breteuil
St Jean de Beauregard
RAMBOUILLET
Courson
Vaux-le-Vicomte
Le Marais
Jeurre
MELUN
PROVINS
Courances
ÈTAMPES
FONTAINEBLEAU
ESSONNE
N
0 km 20

HTS-DE-SEINE
SEINE-St-DENIS
Malmaison
Bagatelle
PARIS
St Cloud
Jardins Kahn
Vincennes
VAL-DE-MARNE
Sceaux
l'Hay-les-Roses
CHATENAY-MALABRY
0 km 10

# PARIS AND THE ILE DE FRANCE

## PARIS

BAGATELLE
Bois de Boulogne, Route de Sèvres à Neuilly, 75016 Paris. Tel: 45 01 20 10.

*In the Bois de Boulogne, off the Allée de Longchamp where it meets the Allée de la Reine Marguerite. There is also an entrance on the Sèvres-Neuilly road. Metro: ligne 1 Porte Maillot - Pont de Neuilly. Bus 244.(35 F3)* **Opening hours:** *Every day. Winter, 9-5; Summer, 9-8. E. Inexpensive. Wheelchairs. Toilets. Restaurant. Bagatelle is deservedly very popular and in high season, visits in the morning or over lunchtime are recommended.*

This lovely garden surrounds the small château that was designed and built in three months by the Comte d'Artois for his sister-in-law, Marie Antoinette. The garden was one of the first *jardins anglais* and was designed by Scottish gardener, Thomas Blaikie, who liked large open grassy spaces and clumps of trees in the manner of Capability Brown. The garden includes a lake bordered by rocks, a winding river and cascades, a Japanese water garden and a formal French *parterre*, which is particularly well planted, as well as the roses for which Bagatelle has become famous. The northern part of the garden, where the rhododendrons and waterlilies are, is very tranquil.

The rose garden has a permanent collection of old roses and species roses grown in grass, climbing and rambling roses grown on pillars, pergolas and arches, as well as the more transient International Concours of Roses in June. A pretty kiosk or pavilion of painted cast-iron lacework, overlooks the rose garden.

Water lilies are a feature from July to September, bulbs from March to April, peonies, lilac, geraniums and clematis between May to September, while from mid-May to mid-June, the iris garden is at its best. There is a particularly attractive garden in which a serpentine box hedge forms small bays that are filled with white, blue and grey plants. A long high wall near the restaurant is covered with clematis, roses and other climbers, with fuchsias and catmint at their feet.

BOIS DE BOULOGNE , PRE CATALAN AND JARDIN SHAKESPEARE
75016 Paris.16th arrondissement.

*In the centre of the Bois between the Route de la Cascade and the Racing Club de France. Well signed. Bus: 244, stop at Parc de Bagatelle. (35 F3)* **Opening hours:** *Pré Catalan, every day 9-sunset; Jardin Shakespeare, 3-3.30 and 4.30-5. E Pré Catalan, free; Jardin Shakespeare, inexpensive. Toilets - public toilets in the Bois. Wheelchairs. Restaurants.*

The Pré Catalan is a large, well kept park with good trees, shrub borders and bedding plants in a French version of the English landscape style.

The Jardin Shakespeare is an open-air theatre that has banked sides to a central stage and auditorium, planted with flowers mentioned in Shakespeare: columbines, marigolds, sages, roses and lavender are just some of the plants growing in the Mediterranean area based on *The Tempest*. There is also a Scottish area for *Macbeth*, a stream for Ophelia, framed in flowering plants chosen from *Hamlet*, a Greek wood from *A Midsummer Night's Dream* and the Forest of Arden. Quite a lot to see in the half hour that it is open!

Much of the Bois de Boulogne's 900 ha is natural woodland and it includes seven waterfalls. Full of joggers and walkers by day, it is not safe at night.

JARDIN DU LUXEMBOURG
Boulevard St Michel, 75006, Paris. 6th arrondissement.

*Metro: Luxembourg. **Opening hours:** Every day 7 or 8-one hour before sunset. E Free. Wheelchairs. Toilets.*

The Luxembourg garden is the largest green space on the Left Bank and on fine days is crowded with students and families with small children.

The gardens have a long history. They were started in 1612 for Marie de Medici, wife of Henry IV, after she was widowed, and were designed to remind her of her youth in Tuscany. In 1630 Marie was banished to Germany because of her opposition to Cardinal Richelieu and the palace reverted eventually to the crown. John Evelyn visited the garden in 1644 and remarked on the exquisite order. After the Revolution the main axis of the *parterre* was extended to the Observatoire with the creation of an avenue, and the gardens were redesigned. The design is still very formal, but much simpler. There are many fine monuments and statues, in particular the Medici Fountain by Salomon de Brosse and the Statue of Liberty by Bartholdi, as well as orangeries and pavilions.

The *ancienne pepinière,* the old nursery garden is now laid out informally as a *jardin anglais.* Fruit trees and glasshouses remain, along with areas for children's games, pony rides and many other attractions.

JARDIN DES PLANTES
57 rue Cuvier, 75005 Paris. 5th arrondissement.

*Metro: Jussieu or Gare d'Austerlitz. **Opening hours:** Every day 7.30-sunset. Winter garden and glasshouses: open 2-5, closed on Tuesdays. Alpine garden: 1 April to 31 October, 10-12 and 2-5, closed on Tuesdays. E. Inexpensive for Winter garden and Alpine garden. Wheelchairs. Toilets.*

The Jardin des Plantes began life as a physic garden in 1626. Medicinal herbs were grown in formal, geometric beds. By the eighteenth century it had become the Jardin Royal des Plantes and many famous naturalists like Buffon and Jussieu were employed there. In the following years it became a centre of plant collecting and expeditions were sent around the world.

Today the garden is more like a park and zoo than a botanic garden although there are order beds belonging to the botanical school which contain more than 10,000 plants. There is a herb garden, an ecological area as well as the alpine garden with more than 2,000 species and the winter garden which contains plants from desert and tropical areas and a small water garden. Tropical and temperate greenhouses have a good collection of exotic plants.

There are some interesting trees, including an *Acer sempervirens* planted in 1702, and the oldest tree in Paris, a *Robinia pseudoacacia* from 1636. A maze on a mound dates from 1640 and has a small belvedere in bronze constructed by Verniquet and Buffon in 1786 at the top.

The Jardin des Plantes is a pleasant place to visit but anyone expecting a garden comaparable to Kew will be disappointed.

JARDINS DES TUILERIES
Place de la Concorde, 75001, Paris. 1st arrondissement.

*Metro: Concorde or Tuileries.* **Opening hours:** *Every day 6 or 6.30-8 or until 11pm according to season. E. Free. Wheelchairs.*

The Jardins des Tuileries is part of the most famous axis in Paris, from the Arc de Triomphe to the Louvre, and possibly the best known open space in France.

Originally created by Catherine de Medici between 1564 and 1572, the gardens were transformed by André le Nôtre in 1666. Le Nôtre's father and grandfather had both been gardeners at the Tuileries. The garden was laid out symmetrically on either side of the main path, the vista was extended, the main *parterre* related to the palace and a terrace walk beside the river Seine was constructed.

The octagonal *bassin* near the Place de la Concorde with its adjoining steps, ramps and terraces is ornamented with many fine statues. A bust of Le Nôtre can be seen to the north of the *bassin* towards the Jeu de Paume. The gardens of the Tuileries are currently undergoing dramatic restoration. Between I. M. Pei's glass pyramid outside the Louvre and the formal quincunxes of trees designed by Le Nôtre there is a large area of lawn surrounded by narrow beds of colorful flowers. Other areas too have been given a softer, 'greener' appearance.

## PARC ANDRE CITROEN
Rue Leblanc, 75015, Paris. 15th arrondissement.

*Metro: Balard.* **Opening hours:** *Every day. E. Free.*

The most exciting new park in Paris is situated where the old Citroen motor works used to be. The ecological influence is striking, as is the 'new age' symbolism of a series of gardens on one side of the site. On the other side, tiers of banked hedges of contrasting color and texture are brilliantly sited against modern reflecting office buildings. There are also glass houses containing Australian plants and black and white gardens. Not to be missed.


## PARC DES BUTTES CHAUMONT
Rue Manin - Rue Crimée. 75019, Paris. 19th arrondissment.

*From the centre of Paris,go in the direction of Meaux, on the N3, to Porte de Pantin, along Rue La Fayette and Avenue Jean Jaurès. 1 km along Avenue Jean Jaurès, turn right into Rue de Crimée. Metro: Botzaris or Buttes Chaumont.* **Opening hours:** *Every day 9-sunset. E .Free. Wheelchairs. Toilets. Three restaurants.*

Before the Second Empire there were no public parks in Paris, although Parisians had used the royal gardens for recreation. It was Napoleon III who, with his engineer Haussmann, designers J.C.A. Alphand and A. Barillet-Deschamps, was responsible for the wide, tree-lined boulevards and the public parks of the Paris we know today.

The park of Buttes-Chaumont was designed and planted by Alphand and Barillet-Deschamps in what was already an open space, but one of rubbish dumps, gibbets and quarries, a sinister area shunned by ordinary people. The designers made good use of the changing levels: they used the rocky mounds as the focal point of the park by digging a lake all round them and building a reproduction of the temple of the Sibyl at Tivoli on top. A footbridge allows access to the island.

Another feature is a 30m cascade that tumbles down inside a cave. This wild park in the picturesque style is one of the most popular parks in Paris. There are also two *guignols* or puppet theatres, bandstands and pony rides.

## PARC MONCEAU
Boulevard de Courcelles, 75008, Paris. 8th arrondissement.

*Metro: Courcelles.* **Opening hours:** *Spring and summer 8am-9pm (11 pm in July and August); autumn and winter 8-8 (7 pm from 1 November to 31 January). E. Free. Wheelchairs. Toilets.*

The Parc Monceau was designed as a *jardin irrégulier* in the English style for the Duke of Chartres, Philippe-Egalité, a dedicated anglophile. It had many follies, some of which remain, including tombs, a pyramid, columns, an arcade, a colonnade and the naumachia, a pool designed to accommodate mock naval battles. It was restored by Alphand during the Second Empire.

There are also roundabouts, games for children of all ages and pony rides.

PARC MONTSOURIS
Boulevard Jourdan, 75014 Paris. 14th arrondissement.

*Metro: Cité Universitaire. Opening hours: Spring and summer 9-9 (10pm from 1 June to 31 August); autumn and winter 9-7 (5.30 in December and January). E ·Free. Wheelchairs. Toilets. Restaurant.*

The Parc Montsouris was created in the south of Paris as part of Napoleon III's vision for the greening of the city. The actual design was J.C.A. Alphand's and had three great lawns planted with trees and shrubs, including sequoias, cedar of Lebanon, poplars from Virgina and elms from Siberia. Many of these trees remain and are now of admirable size.

The main curiosity is the Bardo, a reproduction of the summer palace of the Bey of Tunis that was made for the 1867 Exhibition. This is being restored by the Tunisian government who hope to transform it into a cultural institute.

PARC FLORAL DE VINCENNES
Esplanade du Château, 75012 Paris. Tel: 43 43 92 95.

*In the Bois de Vincennes, not far from the château. Metro: Château de Vincennes. Bus 112. Opening hours: Every day, summer 9-8, winter 9-5.30. E. Free (small charge for certain shows.) Wheelchairs. Toilets. Restaurant.*

This floral park is in the middle of the Bois de Vincennes. It was created as the venue for the third International Floralies in 1969. Between May and September it is also home to clowns, jugglers and buskers of all kinds and is very busy.

The lakes, fountains, modern pavilions and terraces are surrounded by colorful beds of pelargoniums, iris, begonias, marigolds and other half-hardy bedding plants and then by woods underplanted with rhododendrons and azaleas. There are also temporary exhibitions.

Also in the Bois de Vincennes are the garden surrounding the **Ecole Superieure d'Agronomie Tropicale** (Institute of Tropical Agronomic Research) (Open Sundays 2-4) with an avenue like that of the famous ruined city of Angkor Wat, and the **Arboretum d'Ecole du Breuil** (School of Horticulture), Route de la Ferme. (Open every day except Saturday and Sunday 7.30-4.30. Guided visits, 1-5, Monday, Wednesday and Friday.) The arboretum has over 2,000 species of hardy woody plants including 270 rose cultivars, fruit trees and a collection of lilacs.

SERRES D'AUTEUIL
3 Avenue de la Porte d'Auteuil and 1 Avenue Gordon Bennett, 75016 Paris.

*South of the Bois de Boulogne. Metro: ligne 10 Porte d'Auteuil.(35 F3)* **Opening hours:** *Every day; in spring and summer from 10-6 and in autumn and winter, from 10-5. E. Inexpensive.*

A winter garden, a tropical glass house and exhibitions of exotic plants. Look out for the orchids, of which there are more than 600 different species, with 470 species of begonias, crotons and anthuriums.

There are more tropical and equatorial plants at **La Serre des Halles** (Rue Coquillière, Porte du Jour, 75001 Paris)


**ESSONNE**

COURANCES
Courances, 91490 Milly-la-Forêt. Tel: 64 98 41 18.

*18 km west of Fontainebleau and 5 km north of Milly-la-Forêt on the D372. (54 B2)* **Opening hours:** *Saturdays, Sundays and holidays from the first Sunday in April to 2 November, 2-6.30. E Park and château, moderate. Wheelchairs. Toilets.*

Courances

Courances is probably the most beautiful formal garden in France. The first glimpse of the symmetrical canals and the double avenues of planes planted in 1782, is a just indicator of the perfection to come. Beyond them is the château with its two pavilions, the *cour d'honneur* and the horseshoe staircase that is a copy of the one at Fontainebleau.

It is not known whether André le Nôtre created the garden, but his style was certainly its inspiration. The original garden had fallen into disrepair during the nineteenth century and was abandoned for many years. In 1872 it was purchased by the Baron de Haber, the present owner's ancestor, and Achille Duchêne was engaged to restore the garden. He uncovered the long lost *bassins* and redefined the gardens and the park.

The garden is a flawless composition of grass, trees, water and stone. Sparklingly clear springs feed the canals and pools and there is the constant sound of running water, its reflections and ripples. Vistas open up in unexpected, yet always exactly right, places.

On the terrace by the château are two *parterres en broderie* while the terrace balustrade is softened with climbing roses, *R.wichuraiana* and *R.filipes* 'Kiftsgate': frothing round the edge of the château, like the single ruffle on an elegant dress. Beyond the moats, kept full by the water that pours continuously from the mouths of strange gargoyles, an enormous lawn with a rectangular *miroir d'eau* stretches to the horizon. The surrounding woodland is edged by limes and clipped hornbeam, accentuated by white statues placed at regular intervals.

To one side a long and shady *allée* suddenly opens out onto a ten-sided pool, with clipped box buns at every corner. Along the side of the Grand Canal is another opening, a cross-axis and there is the famous water stairway guarded by dogs at one end and a pair of lions at the other. Here the water does not gush, or ripple, but glides slowly over the shallow ledges beneath the dappled shade of the trees.

From the far end of the main vista behind the circular Rond du Moigny, a statue of Hercules standing on a large terrace, looks down towards the château. From here the château is clear, but the garden between is invisible.

On the other side of the château, the east side, Duchêne designed a small half-moon pool into which water flows from over a semi-circular mossy cascade surmounted by a statue of a nymph. Further from the house on this same side is the wonderfully contrasting Japanese garden, made by the current owner's grandmother, Berthe, Marquise de Ganay, between the two wars. This can only be seen from the path as it is too fragile to take many visitors. Red leaved acers contrast with the green trees and the gunnera around the water. A dense planting of hostas, Japanese anemones, ruscus, *Prunus lusitanica* and robinia form a rich tapestry of texture and color.

DOMAINE DE COURSON
91680 Courson Monteloup . Tel: 64 58 90 12.

*35 km south west of Paris. Take the A20 to Etampes and Orleans and Courson is signed from the Arpajon Centre exit towards Limours. Or take the Les Ulis/ Chartres exit from the A10 Chartres autoroute and go towards Monthlery and then Dourdan. (53 F1)* **Opening hours:** *Garden, Sundays and holidays, 10-12 and 2-6. Journées des Plantes de Courson the third weekend in May and October. E. moderate. Toilets. Wheelchairs. (Special visits for the handicapped by arrangement.)*

The park at Courson is a romantic park in the English manner. It replaces a traditional French garden, being first re-designed by Berthault, the landscape gardener who advised Josephine at Malmaison, and later by one of the Bühler brothers. Now replanting is being undertaken to the designs of English landscape designer, Timothy Vaughan. The result is a composite of four different periods of planting.

The original planting was of French forest trees, chestnuts, limes, oaks and beeches, which are now in their full maturity. In 1823, 4,600 new plants arrived, including lilacs, cornuses, genistas, brooms, sorbuses, sumacs, oriental planes, acacias, poplars, willows and catalpas. Three years later, clumps of peonies, rhododendrons and dahlias were planted.

Bühler planted yet more trees, using purple copper beeches and oaks, and also pines, swamp cypresses, tulip trees and giant sequoias. Between 1920-50, the Comte de Caraman, owner of Courson, influenced by his friend Albert Kahn, who created the Jardins Albert Kahn in Paris, planted many conifers, including the weeping blue cedar that hangs over the lake, and completed the planting there of rhododendrons, azaleas and peonies.

Since 1981, Timothy Vaughan has been extending and developing the planting further, with a mixed shrub and rose border in the angle of the château, as well as underplanting groups of trees with amelanchiers, viburnums and cornus. He has also created the Allée de Timothy by planting new *bosquets* of rare small trees and shrubs, such as magnolias, *Cercidiphyllum japonicum,* and enkianthus. One group, of newly planted corylopsis varieties and exochorda, makes an interesting composition for early and late spring.

Details of the spring and autumn plant fairs are regularly announced in the RHS journal 'The Garden'

## PARC DE JEURRE
Morigny Champigny, 91150 Etampes. Tel: 64 94 57 43.

*5 km north of Etampes on the N20, on the right. One of the great arches can be seen first: slow down and look out for the gate. (54 A2)* **Opening hours:** *Every day except Wednesday, Saturday morning, Sundays before holidays and holidays. Guided visits only at 10 and 3.* **E.** *Moderate. Wheelchairs, with difficulty.*

La Laiterie, Parc de Jeurre

Jeurre is a strange, romantic, overgrown park and the interest is in the *fabriques* brought here from other buildings, destroyed or abandoned. The château of Jeurre was ornamented by the great grandfather of the present proprietor, using façades from buildings being demolished - the Hotel de Madame de Pompadour in the Rue Ménars in Paris and the Hotel d'Anglade from the Rue des Archives. The other buildings and artefacts in the garden come from Méréville and St Cloud.

Méréville had been created between 1784 and 1793 by the Marquis de Laborde, banker to the court; Hubert Robert painter and landscape designer, Belanger who designed Bagatelle and Barré, who designed Le Marais, were responsible for the design. Laborde was guillotined in 1794 during the Revolution and the estate was bought in 1824 by the Comte de Saint-Roman but on his death was divided into lots and sold. The Temple de la Piété Filiale, one of the finest park monuments in France, the façade of the Laiterie, the rostral column and Cook's cenotaph were removed from Méréville and re-erected at Jeurre. This took over fifteen years.

The guided tour goes first by the Colonne Rostrale which commemorates the La Pérouse expedition to the Pacific on 1 August 1785. The *communs* or outbuildings are in the style of farmhouses of northern Italy, a contrast to the château with its borrowed classical façades. A seventeenth century armillary sphere on a column of pink granite can be seen across a small river. At the back of the château are a rectangular pool, two *sphinges*, borders of roses and arrangement of urns and statues. At the end of the pool is the façade of the Laiterie.

The imposing Cook monument is next on the tour, with its inscribed poems by l'Abbé de Lisle. At the end of a long grassy walk through the woods is a huge arch that was part of the front of the left wing of the Château of St Cloud which was burnt down in 1870 during the siege of Paris. The principal *allée* has a gate that came from the Hôtel of the Comtesse de Verrue but unfortunately the stone is crumbling. This is the gate that can be seen from the N20 and warns the visitor that the entrance to Jeurre is near.

There is a green walk round the back of the rostral column on the return journey and a pigeon house like a tower can be seen behind the outbuildings. The circular Temple de la Piété Filiale, with a statue of Venus inside, stands in a meadow surrounded by huge blue cedars and green limes. This is a garden that is of particular interest to garden historians and architects.

LE MARAIS
Saint Chéron, 91530 Val-Saint-Germain. Tel: 64 58 96 01.

*Leave the A10 autoroute from Paris to Chartres at the Dourdan exit, and go towards Rochefort-en-Yveslines. Turn to the right on the D27 in the direction of Arpajon and Le Marais is 8 km. (53 F1)* **Opening hours:** *15 March to 15 November, Sundays and holidays 2-6.30. E. Garden only, very moderate. Toilets. Wheelchairs.*

As its name suggests, Le Marais is built on marshy land and the garden is a simple one of grass and water. The *cour d'honneur* and the château are surrounded by moats, as are the outbuildings, while the best known feature of the garden is the enormous *miroir d'eau* between the gate of the château and the road. The simple lawn at the back of the garden is bisected by a narrow rill and has a pool in the middle. It was reconstructed by Henri and

Achille Duchêne. There are walks in the woods, which are carpeted in spring with periwinkles and wood anemones.

## ST JEAN DE BEAUREGARD
91940 St-Jean-de-Beauregard. Tel: 60 12 00 01.

*Leave Paris on the A10 to Chartres and take Exit Les Ulis. Take D35, direction Chartres, to Gometz and Limours and before Gometz, turn sharp left back to Villeziers and St Jean. (35 F4)* **Opening hours:** *15 March to 15 November, Sundays and holidays, 2-6. E. Park and potager moderate. Wheelchairs. Toilets.*

The imposing Louis XIII château has a fine *parterre* of pink roses and clipped box in a *fleur de lys* pattern in front, separated from it by a precise strip of box in a trellis pattern, a balustrade and a double flight of steps. The château is surrounded by a wooded park. A large dovecote with spaces for 4,000 birds is now used as a visitor centre.

To gardeners however, the most exciting part of the garden is the *potager*, still containing traces of the original garden which used to support a household of 20 or 30 people in the seventeenth and eighteenth centuries. Vegetables and fruit are still grown, and stored in traditional storage buildings, but all round the edge of the garden are herbaceous plants - mallows, hostas, campanulas, white *Salvia sclarea turkestanica*, and day lilies. Box-edged beds, which used to contain vegetables, are full of rows of flowers for cutting for the house while by the greenhouse is a collection of old roses, with climbers and rambler roses growing over a pergola.

A central pool is surrounded by peonies and there is also a peony walk planted at the beginning of the century, with peonies down one side and currant bushes down the other, in true *potager* style. More peonies and irises are grown in front of a row of espaliered pear trees while four large beds of vegetables containing a hundred different cultivars are still to be seen around the central pond. The herb bed contains medicinal and aromatic plants as well as culinary herbs. Raspberries, handsome, grey-leaved artichokes, plums and sinuous vines all add to the sense of richness and profusion of this extensive *potager*.

There is a sale of herbaceous plants every year in April and a display and sale of old vegetable varieties each November.

## HAUTS DE SEINE

## JARDINS ALBERT KAHN
14 rue du Port, 92100 Boulogne-Billancourt. Tel: 46 04 52 80.

*The Jardins Kahn are between the Quai du 4-septembre and the Rue des Abondances close to the River Seine almost opposite St Cloud and very close to the the Pont de*

*St Cloud. Metro: Boulogne-Pont de Saint-Cloud, Rhin et Danube.* **Opening hours:** *Every day except Monday, 1 May to 30 September, 11-7; 1 October to 30 April, 11-6. Wheelchairs. Toilets. Salon du Thé.* **E.** *Inexpensive.*

These gardens were created between 1900 and 1913 by Albert Kahn, a banker and keen amateur horticulturist. The ensemble comprises a blue garden with a framework of *Cedrus atlantica glauca*, underplanted with hydrangeas, hostas and *Festuca glauca*; an English garden with limes, planes, sycamores and a ginkgo; a formal French garden, a fruit and rose garden and a golden garden as well as an area like that of the forests of the Vosges. Huge trees of 15-20 metres high were transported in enormous waggons to create an instant forest in 1910. The gardens have been meticulously restored recently.

In the fruit and rose garden, traditionally trained apple, pear and quince trees support a collection of climbing roses. The original Japanese village with its thatched tea house has been restored and there is a completely new modern Japanese garden that symbolises the life and philosophy of Albert Kahn. There are a brilliant lacquer red replica of the sacred bridge of Nikko, a mound of clipped azaleas which represents Mount Fuji, miniature rice terraces, and ever-present water, sometimes calm, sometimes turbulent, mirroring the life of the garden's creator.

One of Albert Kahn's many projects was to send photographers round the world from 1902 on to capture the life of ordinary people on film. These photographs are on exhibition in a splendid new gallery. The palmarium, an enormous and elaborate glasshouse is now the Salon du Thé.

MALMAISON
Avenue du Château, 92500 Rueil-Malmaison. Tel: 47 29 20 07.

*On the N13 which hugs the River Seine between St Germain, Le Pecq, le Port Marly and Rueil-Malmaison. Well signed in Rueil-Malmaison. RER ligne St Germain. (35 F3)* **Opening hours:** *All year from 10-12 and 1.30-4.30 (5 in winter)* **E.** *Inexpensive. Wheelchairs. Toilets.*

Malmaison was the favourite house of the Empress Josephine who had spent some of her happiest hours there with Napoleon before he became Emperor. After their divorce, she lived there again until her death in 1843.

The garden used to cover 726 ha and included a model farm and a famous hot-house. These no longer exist and the area of the garden is now much smaller. The rose garden is a rectangular area divided into triangles around a central circle of grass. Portland and Provins roses, together with centifolias and damasks, are well represented as are several that recall Josephine, including 'Chapeau de Napoleon' and Vibert's 'Cuisse de Nymphe Emué'. A great deal of imagination is necessary to reconcile the conception of

Malmaison as it must have been with the reality today. For the gardener and rose lover, the garden at Bagatelle and the rosery at l'Hay les Roses are to be preferred.

## ARBORETUM DEPARTEMENTAL DE LA VALLEE-AUX-LOUPS
46 rue de Chateaubriand, 92290 Chatenay-Malabry. Tel: 41 13 00 90

*10 km south of Paris, part of the Vallée aux Loups park to the east of Sceaux. From Paris, take N20 to Etampes across Porte d'Orleans. After 11 km turn onto the N186 to Versailles and Châtenay Malabry. After 3 km turn into D26 towards Fontenay au Roses and the hamlet of Aulnay. This garden was originally part of the neighbouring Pepinières Croux but is now only open for groups during the week and by appointment.*

A richly planted landscape garden next door to the nursery founded by M. Croux in 1890. It has been planned so that a walk round the sinuous lake, with its bridges and summerhouse, gives many different views and seems to increase the apparent size of the garden.

There are some exceptional trees, which were planted at the end of the last century: a *Taxodium distichum nutans* by the lake, with roots rising to an enormous height out of the water, *Populus szechuanica,* with handsome leaves; a cedar of Lebanon planted in 1730, a golden yew from the same century and a magnificent blue cedar. The trees are underplanted with azaleas, kalmias, heathers, hostas and berberis.

## ST CLOUD
92210 St Cloud. Tel: 46 02 70 01.

*12 km west of Paris. Leave the A13 Paris to Rouen road at St Cloud. Metro: Pont de St-Cloud. (35 F4) **Opening hours:** Every day 7 or 8am to 9 or 10pm according to season. The famous cascades and the 24 jets are switched on only on the second and fourth Sunday of each month between May and September, 4-5. E.Free but there is a small charge for cars which is worthwhile as the area is enormous. Wheelchairs. Toilets.*

There was a notable garden at St Cloud that had been praised by John Evelyn well before it was bought by Louis XIV's brother, Monsieur, the Duke of Orleans, in 1658. André le Nôtre was called in to redesign the gardens and then, on the occasion of Monsieur's second marriage, to Elisabeth-Charlotte of Bavaria, the château was enlarged by Hardouin-Mansart and he also enlarged the Grande Cascade at the same time. Queen Victoria once stayed there and thought the view of Paris 'splendid', which it still is, encompassing the Eiffel tower and the dome of the Sacré Coeur.

The château was burnt to the ground during the Franco-Prussian war of 1870 and its site is now marked out by conical yews. The gardens with their straight *allées*, the great horseshoe shaped vista, the Fer à cheval, are cut out of the forest and the trees, a green wall of chestnuts, stand at the edge of the grass rides, looking as if they are waiting to return. The area where the château was sited is surrounded by statues, standing at the edge of the trees. The Jet de la Grande Gerbe is behind the château site. One of its fountains shoots water 40 feet in the air, while the canals by the side, have 24 fountain jets. These, and the Grande Cascade, work occasionally. The Grande Cascade is slightly to the west, between the area of the château and the Seine, and has three slopes, stepped with *bassins* and vases, separated by two arched grottoes.

The park also contains box-edged beds of mosaiculture, while the surrounding woods have picnic areas, and many fine rides and vistas.

SCEAUX
92330 Sceaux. Tel: 46 61 06 71.

*Leave Paris by Porte d'Orleans, direction Chartres. Sceaux is 5 km and is west of the N20. From Versailles take A86 direction Creteil, and turn left on to N20 at Place General de Gaulle. (35 F4).* **Opening hours:** *Every day, 7 (8 in winter)-sunset. E. Free. Toilets. Wheelchairs.*

In 1670 Louis XIV's minister, Colbert, acquired the château of Sceaux and immediately set about embellishing and enlarging it. André le Nôtre, the designer of Vaux-le-Vicomte and Versailles was the obvious choice to redesign the gardens. Colbert learned from the bitter story of Nicholas Fouquet at Vaux, and was careful to decorate the entrance pavilion with statues by Coysevox of a dog and unicorn, both symbols of loyalty and fidelity that he knew Louis XIV would recognise.

The garden had two main axes, the Grand Canal and the Plaine des Quatres Statues, which converged at right angles on the château. The original château was demolished in 1798 and rebuilt in a fake Louis XIII style in 1856. It now houses the very interesting Musée de l'Ile de France which has been restored and was reopened to the public in May 1994. The axis down to the Plaine, dotted with small conical yews, ends suddenly at some busy roads and is disappointing but the Grand Canal axis is quite another matter.

A whole chain of formal cascades (a modern reconstruction of the original) links the house above to a great octagonal pool which in its turn is connected to the main canal. This is one of Le Nôtre's greatest triumphs, showing his mastery of an awkward, steep site. The huge sheet of water is surrounded by statues and curtains of plane trees, making a well defined space that is both enclosed and expansive. Splendid *allées* are cut through the trees to the Grand Canal.

The Pavillon d'Aurore, a rotunda with a dome painted by Le Brun, is the one garden building that still survives from the time of Colbert. The lovely Orangery, designed for Colbert's son by the architect Hardouin-Mansart, is used for exhibitions and concerts. The other building in the garden, the Pavillon du Hanovre, was originally sited in the Boulevard des Italiens but was moved to Sceaux in 1930. The whole site is well maintained by the Conseil General des Hauts de Seine which has owned it since 1971.

VALLEE AUX LOUPS , MAISON DE CHATEAUBRIAND
87 rue de Chateaubriand, 92290 Chatenay-Malabry. Tel: 47 29 30 31.

*10 km south of Paris. Leave by Porte d'Orleans, N20 Direction Etampes. At the Croix de Berny, turn right to Versailles and Chatenay Malabry on N186. (35 F4).* **Opening hours:** *1 April to 30 September, 10-12 and 2-6; 1 October to 31 March, 1.30-4.30. Closed on Mondays. Tuesdays and Thursdays are reserved for groups and for those who have made an appointment. E. Gardens inexpensive, guided tours of house, plus grounds, moderate. Toilets (down stairs in the museum.) Wheelchairs.*

The house where Chateaubriand lived for ten years between 1807 and 1817 and where he wrote the first chapters of his greatest work 'Mémoires d'Outre-Tombe', has been wonderfully restored by the Regional Council of Hauts-de-Seine, to become yet again, a cultural centre for the region.

Chateaubriand was captivated by the wild nature of the valley when he first saw it and the simple brewer's house and garden was transformed by the spirit of Romanticism that held sway after the Revolution. A portico was added to the façade of the house, supported by black marble columns and two white caryatids and the garden was turned into a *jardin irregulier*, a garden in which a framed view changes into a series of scenes that you participate in as you walk along the winding paths.

The last stage of the restoration is that of the Tower of Velleda in the woods. There is also an ice house. The park was planted with trees that reminded Chateaubriand of his childhood home in Brittany, the Château of Combourg, and to evoke an imaginary journey: the oaks of Gaul, the cedars of the Orient and magnolias and bald cypressses (*Taxodium distichum* or swamp cypress) from America. There are also catalpas, including one large one planted by Chateaubriand himself, rhododendrons, copper beeches and a belt of chestnuts.

Even in March heathers softly color the flower bed round the orangery and dazzling white crocuses sparkle on the gently sloping lawn. The attractive orangery is perhaps best seen when the overhanging trees are without their leaves, but it is generally said that the garden is at its best in either May and June, when the rhododendrons are in flower, or in the autumn when the trees are changing color.

## SEINE ET MARNE

### CHAMPS
77420 Champs-sur-Marne Tel: 60 05 24 43.

*From Paris, at Porte de Bercy take motorway A4 twoards Marne-la-Vallée (Nancy-Metz). Take exit to Champs. The château is well signed. (36 B3)* **Opening hours:** *Garden opens at 9.30 and closes at 7.30 in May and June, at 8 in July and August, at 7 in September, at 6 in October, at 5 in November; at 4.30 between 1 December and 20 February; 21 February to 20 March, at 5.30 and at 6.30 between 21 March and 30 April. The château is closed on Tuesdays and 12-1.30. E. Park free. Wheelchairs. Toilets.*

Designed by Claude Desgots a nephew of Le Nôtre, this splendid formal garden with its magnificent symmetries was restored by Henri and Achille Duchêne around 1900. It is noted for its long sloping *parterre en broderie* in clipped box and a magnificent central vista, its circular pools lively with fountains, which ends with a double-size copy of the sculpture The Horses of Apollo at Versailles.

Narrow pyramids of yew, red roses and double avenues of clipped hornbeam, all beautifully maintained, add just enough color, height and liveliness to invigorate the formal design.

Desgots can not have known that Paris was going to creep round this château, with motorways, hectic traffic, ugly tower blocks and factories, but if he had deliberately set out to provide a contrast, a sanctuary where all was harmonious, orderly and in scale he could not have done it better. There are few more difficult places to get to on the outskirts of Paris but none where the whole concept of the French formal garden seems, because of its surroundings, to have such clarity. The effort of getting there is well worth while.

### CHATEAU DE FERRIERES
77164 Ferrières. Tel: 64 30 31 25.

*Very near the A4, 25 km east of Paris towards Reims. Leave the A4 at the Lagny-Melun exit and go towards Melun. Turn off the N371 to D35 to Lagny and Ferrières. (36 B3)* **Opening hours:** *1 May to 30 September, every day except Monday and Tuesday, 2-7; 1 October to 30 April, Saturday, Sunday and Wednesday, 2-5. E. To park, inexpensive. Wheelchairs. Toilets in château.*

Château de Ferrières

The great block of the Château of Ferrières was designed for Baron James de Rothschild by Joseph Paxton, the gardener of Chatsworth and designer of the Crystal Palace.

The garden was also designed by Paxton and is in the English landscape style and contains many fine trees. Near the house is an arrangement of square clipped yews with a monumental bulk that echoes that of the building. Close by the large leaves of a golden catalpa and a *Magnolia grandiflora*, contrast with the neatly textured yew. From the terrace the lawns slope away to a serpentine lake with willowed banks and small islands and the natural park with its copper beeches and blue cedars. Near the lake, *Liriodendron tulipferum, Tilia americana* and a *Magnolia x soulangeana* make an interesting group.

Great clumps of giant sequoias grow on one side of the park while on the other an entire border of rugosa roses edges the path to the Fontaine des Quatre Saisons. The tiny Ile d'Amour that juts out into the lake is surrounded by three weeping trees - a sophora, a silver lime and an ash. The Japanese garden at the end of the lake is rather neglected and the alpine garden is unexciting.

FONTAINEBLEAU
77300 Fontainbleau. Tel: 64 22 27 40.

*65 km south of Paris on the N7 or the A8. (54 C2)* **Opening hours:** *Every day, 8-sunset. (The Jardin Anglais and the Jardin de Diane close one hour before sunset.)* **E.** *Free access to grounds. Toilets (adapted for the disabled). Wheelchairs.*

The entrance court to the Palace of Fontainebleau, with the striking horseshoe staircase, is as splendid as the rich history of the building. Beyond it, the second courtyard, the Cour de la Fontaine, overlooks the great carp pond with what must be one of the largest masses of hungry, writhing carp ever. To the right of this lake, which has a pretty pavilion on an island, is the *jardin anglais*. This was designed in 1811 and was planted with specimen trees in part of what had been the *Jardin des Pins*. The only part of this now remaining is the *Grotte du Jardin des Pins*, three rusticated arches containing statues of Juno and Minerva in fresco and a fountain. This feature has been restored recently and is worth seeking out.

To the left of the carp pond is the enormous *parterre* designed by Le Nôtre between 1661 and 1664. This is the largest *parterre* he designed but today, without its patterning of clipped box, it is uninteresting. Although surrounded by double rows of trained trees, there is no sense of enclosure and the conical yews are much too small for the area they are meant to adorn. The magnificent walls of trees that can be seen at Sceaux and Versailles are absent here. Happily this *parterre* is to be restored so that it more approximates to the original design.

The N6 cuts across the garden but does not visually disturb the vista from the *parterre*. Beyond the road, the Grand Canal stretches away between rows of lime trees. Overlooking the road and facing away from the *parterre* is an architectural cascade, with statues in niches round the sides.

To the north of the palace is the Jardin de Diane. This was originally a private garden with access only from the royal apartments. It has been through several transformations, including having a *parterre en broderie* designed by Le Nôtre, but the present style is from the time of Louis-Philippe. In the middle is a statue of Diana the huntress attended by four urinating hounds.

ROSERAIE J VIZIER
11 Rue des Prés, 77160 Provins. Tel: 64 00 02 42.

*Go west from St Ayoul church. Take first right (Ave du Souvenir) then first left. Follow the signs to Roseraie via the Boulevard d'Aligré. Signed also from the Place du Chatel.(55 E1)* **Opening hours:** *Every day except Sunday, 8-12 and 1-5.30.* **E.** *Free. Wheelchairs.*

A rose garden attached to the nursery of the late rose grower, J. Vizier containing some old roses, including, of course the Provins rose, *Rosa gallica*. In the thirteenth century, the petals of *R.gallica* were widely used in pot pourri and preserves and Provins became prosperous from rose growing. The town was surrounded by fields of gallicas. M. Vizier's nursery garden is on a much smaller scale but rose lovers should find it of interest.

If you have time, continue along the Boulevard d'Aligré, the shady promenade along the canal bank. Turn to the right and a short way down is the **Jardin Garnier** (Open 1 October to 3 March, 8-7 on Wednesday and Saturday and 8-6 for rest of the week. 1 April to 30 September, 8-8 every day.) This is an amazing example of a French municipal park as it contains a bit of everything and is done with great panache. There are bold beds of brilliant bedding plants cut out of the grass, a tiny exotic garden with cactus, aloes and huge palms in pots; there are grottoes, streams, a lake with a bridge, and a tiny water wheel which keeps the water on the move, statues, trained trees, a little topiary cat and a bear, as well as roses, conifers, acers and other plants. This 'quart in a pint pot' surrounds the Villa Garnier, which is now the public library.

VAUX LE VICOMTE
77950 Maincy. Tel: 64 14 41 90. Fax: 60 69 90 85.

*5 km from Melun, north east on the N36 and then D215 (54 C1). Opening hours: 1 April to 31 October, every day 10-6; November to March, telephone for information. Fountains are working on the second and last Saturday of each month, from April to October, 3-6. E. Park and gardens only, moderate. Wheelchairs. Toilets (adapted for the disabled.) Restaurant.*

Vaux-le-Vicomte was André le Nôtre's first great masterpiece. It was built for Louis XIV's minister of finances, Nicolas Fouquet, who celebrated its completion with a splendid party, complete with fireworks and an entertainment by Molière, to which he invited Louis. The king examined the garden from every viewpoint but his behaviour to his minister was somewhat cool and soon afterwards Fouquet was arrested and charged with high treason and embezzlement. For a minister of finances to be able to build and to entertain on such a lavish scale was probably evidence of malpractice and certainly of presumption. The unfortunate Fouquet spent the rest of his life in jail.

Louis then decided to use the same partnership of Le Nôtre, the architect Le Vau and designer Le Brun to build an even more splendid palace for himself, and the result was Versailles. Many of the statues were removed from Vaux and were re-erected there.

After this inauspicious beginning, Fouquet's heirs were ruined and the garden was more or less abandoned. In 1875 it was bought by Alfred

Sommier, a wealthy sugar beet merchant. His great-nephew and his son were responsible for having it classified as an ancient monument and for its subsequent restoration by Achille Duchêne. In spite of its being a complete reconstruction - Louis had taken 1,200 of the trees to Versailles along with the statues, and what remained had fallen into disrepair - this is today one of the finest classical French gardens.

Immediately outside the château is an elaborate *parterre en broderie* picked out in red and black gravel. A circular *bassin* with a fountain and two narrow canals overlooks a simpler *parterre* with symmetrical pools. The magnificent main axis continues beyond the gentle slope down to the river Anqueuil which was enlarged to make the Great Canal of nearly 1 km long, through a narrowing *allée* and up to the Farnese statue of Hercules almost on the horizon. But this is a garden full of surprises. The plan is not exactly symmetrical, there is a slight fall across the site and because of the changing levels of the ground, many of the cross axes are not revealed until they are reached. The same is true of the Grand Canal which crosses the garden. The cascades, too, are invisible from the château. Mid-way along the main axis however, from the balustrade above the grottoes on the far side of the canal, the cascades make a perfectly proportioned foreground to a view of the château some distance behind.

The enormous size of the statue of Hercules is not appreciated until it is reached by quite a long walk but from there one can look back to the château and, when the weather is right, see it perfectly reflected in the rectangular *miroir d'eau.*

The cross axes increase in length as they become distant from the house. The distance between them increases too and these characteristics, together with the placing of the enclosing, dense woodland, creates false perspectives and foreshortening. Statues of river gods, *bassins*, pavilions, bridges are invisible until one is almost upon them. This is the garden to visit to really appreciate Le Nôtre's skill with perspective and his use of the elements of surprise and variety inside a very formal structure.


## VAL DE MARNE

### ROSERAIE DE L'HAY-LES-ROSES
Rue Albert Watel, 94240 l'Haÿ-les-Roses. Tel: 47 40 04 04.

*L'Hay -les-Roses is south of Paris via Porte d'Italie. Metro: Bourg-la-Reine - Ligne de Sceaux - and then bus 192. Bus: Porte d'Orleans 187 and Porte d'Italie 286.(35 F4)* **Opening hours:** *Mid-May until mid-September, 10-8.30. E. Inexpensive. Wheelchairs. Toilets at entrance to park.*

No gardener or flower lover should miss the Roseraie, tucked away on its triangular site in the corner of a larger municipal park. The sight of pergolas and trellis-work swagged and swathed with old fashioned ramblers like 'Sanders' White', 'Alberic Barbier', 'Evangeline', 'Dorothy Perkins' and 'American Pillar' is stunning, especially when combined with beds of the latest fluorescent hybrid teas. The eyes can be rested, however, and the pace varied, by leisurely examination of the more specialised collections.

This rose garden is correctly described as the 'living history of the rose' and no one, from the complete novice to the most expert of rose growers, could fail to find it absorbing. Not only are there dozens of unusual varieties, new and old, but they are grown in many different ways - as standards, climbers trained on trellis or along ropes, as shrubs and espaliers. 'Mrs John Lang', 'Paul Neyron' and 'Baron Girod de l'Ain' are used as single tier espaliers to edge beds of shrub roses.

There is one long walk devoted to the history of the rose, spanning the ages, from wild roses to those of today; there is a bed devoted to the roses of Malmaison with their lovely names, 'Belle Aurore', 'Thalis la Gentille', 'Euphrosine', another to the ancient roses of Asia. A central decorative area has a pool, statues and trellis-work surrounded by pillar roses like 'Phyllis Bide' and 'Ghislaine de Feligonde', an attractive apricot-budded rambler that fades to white. In addition there is a collection of old roses that were never grown commercially and a section devoted to new foreign roses.

The botanical section has collections of rugosa roses and what are labelled *rosier pimprenelles* (Scotch roses). A splendid collection of gallicas includes 'Gros Provins Panaché' and 'Madame Legras de St Germain' as well as the better known 'Jacques Cartier', 'Fantin la Tour' and 'Madame Hardy'.

## VAL D'OISE

CHATEAU D'AMBLEVILLE
95710 Bray-et-Lû. Tel: 34 67 71 34.

*12 km from Giverny and 60 km from Paris. Take the N14 from Pontoise to Magny-en-Vexin. At Magny, take the D86 towards Vernon. The château is on the right after several kilometres. (35 D2)* **Opening hours:** *15 April to 15 October, Saturday and Sunday 10.30-6.30. E. Moderate.*

The Italian gardens at Ambleville were created by the present owner's grandmother, the Marquise de Villefranche, who, while living nearby at Villarceaux, bought Ambleville between the two world wars. The first terrace is inspired by the famous garden of the Villa Gamberaia at Fiesole in Italy.

At one end of the garden, a pierced yew hedge forms a background for statues and a hemispherical *bassin*. A central circular pool with a *manneken pis* fountain is surrounded by clipped evergreen shrubs and the whole is under the stern gaze of a bust of Vitellius. A second, higher terrace has a fine serpentine box hedge, one end of which is trimmed to the shape of the serpent's head. Three huge yew trees are trained to the shape of chess pieces while further hedges represent the rays of the sun. A cascade joins the two levels. The whole of the garden is rich with Italian Renaissance symbolism. Blue and white pots containing citrus trees and a shrub border with some grey leaved shrubs depart from the purely Italian ingredients of stone, water and evergreens.

## PAVILLON CHINOIS DE CASSAN
95290 L'Isle-Adam.

*Leave Autoroute A16 at exit L'Isle Adam. In town take the road to Beaumont-sur-Oise, the N322. (35 F2)* **Opening hours:** *Every day, permanently. E. Free.*

This startlingly exotic construction, a two-storied pagoda on a stone plinth with a pillared, slightly sunken colonnade beneath, stands in a small public park planted with azaleas and tall sycamores, by the edge of the road.

The Pavillon was restored in 1975 and from the gallery, one can see the beautifully decorated interior and look out over a pleasant lake and park. The Château of Cassan was damaged in World War II and then parts of the grounds were sold off in separate lots. The best view of this important piece of eighteenth century chinoiserie, from the other side of the lake, is irretrievably lost to the general public for in the resulting development of little villas, not even a footpath to the edge of the lake has been retained.

## CHATEAU DE VILLARCEAUX
95710 Chaussy. Tel: 34 67 75 07.

*Take the D37 from Vernon to Magny en Vexin, 60 km north west of Paris. At Bray-et-Lû take the D142 south east to Chaussy. (35 D2). The estate came under the umbrella of the Conseil Régional d'Ile de France and they plan to make it an international centre for the Art of Gardens. No information on opening hours has been forthcoming but it is certainly worth the brief detour from Ambleville or Giverny to take a chance of seeing the gardens.*

The narrow empty roads, gentle wooded hills and parkland of the Epte valley seem an unlikely setting for the formal Italian garden, dating from the time of François I in the first half of the sixteenth century.

Villarceaux has one of the earliest Italian gardens in France. In the mid seventeenth century it was owned by Louis de Mornay, a master of wolfhounds to the king. One of his most famous mistresses was Ninon de l'Enclos. This celebrated courtesan lived at Villarceaux during the summer of 1654 in the little tower on the east façade of the manor which has a panoramic view of the water garden. One of the many pools, filled by an elegant water staircase from the lake, is known as the Bain de Ninon.

## YVESLINES

### CHATEAU DE BRETEUIL
Choisel, 78460 Chevreuse. Tel: 30 52 05 02.

*Between Versailles and Rambouillet. Leave Versailles by the D91 Vallée de Chevreuse road. Turn left for St Forget and Chevreuse at Dampierre and then take the N306 south of Chevreuse. Breteuil is very well signed.(35 E4)* **Opening hours:** *Every day. The park from 10, the château from 2.30 until sunset. E. Park moderate. Toilets. Wheelchairs, most is accessible.*

The gardens at Breteuil were designed by Henri Duchêne and his son Achille, after the style of Le Nôtre, in about 1900. Designs for their *parterres* can still be seen on the walls of the Orangery. The formal gardens with the *miroir d'eau* , traditional obelisks of clipped yew and buns of trimmed box perfectly set off the château. There is a mediaeval dovecote, an ice house and a fine cedar carpeted around with cyclamen.

The new Jardin des Princes is a mixture of French formality and English planting. On one side is a pergola covered with old roses, on the other an *allée* of traditionally trained fruit trees. A collection of tree peonies has been rescued from near Orleans, and is now to be found at Breteuil in the new garden. There are marked paths through the surrounding woods of old chestnut and holly trees to two lakes, one with an island, planted with water lilies, and edged with bamboo and a variety of shrubs.

### JARDIN DES BRONZES COUBERTIN
Domaine de Coubertin, 78470 St Rémy-lès-Chevreuse. Tel: 30 85 69 89.

*Turn left (south) off the road between St Rémy-lès-Chevreuse and Chevreuse: signed Fondation Coubertin and Atelier St Jacques. On reaching the gates, turn again and then keep right into the Fondation.(35 E4)* **Opening hours:** *Two months each autumn, from mid-September to mid-November, except Monday and Tuesday, 2-6, for the annual sculpture exhibition, and for pre-arranged visits by groups at other times. E.Very moderate.*

The major part of the Fondation Coubertin, housed in the château and its buildings, is a world renowned foundry for the casting of bronze sculptures and the most important part of the garden is that section especially designed to display changings pieces of sculpture.

In front of the early eighteenth century château, an enormous bronze horse by Bourdelle may compete for attention with a group of twelve feet high conical yews but the following year the picture can be entirely different.

The Jardin des Bronzes was created in 1980-1 by the architect and designer, Robert Auzelle, on the site of the old *potager* to the right of the château. The bronzes, from the French school of 1850-1950, are displayed in a modern, geometric layout of concrete slabs and gravel, with different levels, stairs and low walls. A small rill with pools at either end forms an axis down the centre of the garden and planting is very low key, deliberately made subordinate to the sculptures.

PARC FLORAL DU CHATEAU DE DAMPIERRE
78270 Dampierre-en-Yveslines. Tel: 30 52 52 64 (Parc Floral.)

*Take the road from Rambouillet to Chevreuse, the N306, then the left fork, the D91, to Dampierre. The Château de Dampierre is in the centre of the village while there is another entrance to the Parc Floral, well signed, on the outskirts of the village towards les Vaux de Cernay. (35 E4). Opening hours: Parc Floral every day April to 15 October, 11-7; château, 1 April to 15 October 2-6 but closed on Tuesdays. E. Parc Floral, expensive; gardens of château, inexpensive. (Concessions for visits to both château and Parc Floral.) Wheelchairs. Toilets. Café.*

The Parc Floral at Dampierre was designed by Johannes Matthijsse who was responsible for the gardens at the Court d'Aron in the Vendée.

In the spring, over 100 varieties of daffodils and hyacinths, the gift of Dutch bulb growers, and interesting collections of smaller bulbs, brighten the gardens. Wild primroses are thick on the grass walk that leads to the château. These are followed by massed arrays of fibrous begonias. Visitors to the garden in May will find drifts of *Meconopsis betonicifolia* and the tulips at their best. In high summer, great displays of cleomes, busy lizzies, eremurus, lilies and irises quite take the breath away. In shady areas, foxgloves and columbines abound. A small stream is thickly edged with *Iris ensata (kaempferi)*.

There are mixed borders as well, with old roses growing amongst the herbaceous perennials, formal rose beds, a pick-your-own-lilies area and a flowering meadow.

All this planting takes place in the farthest reaches of the romantic park which extends beyond the formal Le Nôtre garden of the Château de Dampierre. A walk past a pavilion and a lake leads eventually to the little kiosk that guards the entrance to the château gardens. Guided visits to the château last about half an hour. At the end of the visit, the formal gardens can be seen, although a good view of the broad sweep of Le Nôtre's design can be obtained from the hill on the other side of the road from the main gates. The château was rebuilt by Hardouin-Mansart between 1675 and 1686. The *parterres, bassins* and cascades are orientated on an axis across the valley and this axis is extended through the richly wooded park at each end.

DESERT DE RETZ
78240 Chambourcy. Tel: 39 76 90 37.

*25 km south of Paris via A13. Leave at exit Poissy-Villennes. Then go towards Orgeval; turn left to St Germain and Chambourcy. In the village take the Allée Frédéric-Passy to the Désert. (35 E3)* **Opening hours:** *Tours at 2.30 and 4 on fourth Saturday of each month from March to October.*

The désert or wilderness of Retz was one of the oddest and most famous of the Anglo-Chinese gardens that were created in eighteenth century France. Like the gardens at Chanteloup and Cassan, where only the Pagoda and the Pavilion remain to indicate past glories, many of the buildings have disappeared or are in ruins. However, for several years now it has been in the process of a very careful restoration by M.Olivier Choppin de Janvry.

Its original creator, the Baron de Monville was influenced by the writings of Sir William Chambers and the fashion for all things Chinese that swept Europe in the second half of the eighteenth century. He purchased land adjoining the forest of Marly and then did not hesitate to ask the king if he could make a gateway through to the royal domain, in order to be able to give the king a better welcome. The entrance is through a primitive grotto made from a vast heap of rocks, and there was a route that passed buildings of many different styles, a Chinese house, a Pyramid, the genuine Gothic ruins of the old village church, a Temple of Pan and an amphitheatre, all set in a picturesque landscape of rocks and trees, that one visitor compared to the 'Grande Chartreuse'.

The Baron de Monville's house was concealed inside an enormous fluted column. The restoration of this is almost complete and inside is an exhibition of plans and drawings. The Turkish tent has been reinstated adding another exotic note to this fascinating garden.

PARC DE MARLY
78430 Louveciennes. Tel: 36 69 06 26 (Musée-Promenade)

*At Marly-le-Roi. Take the A13 towards Versailles-west in the direction of St Germain.* **Opening hours:** *Every day, permanently. E. Free. Wheelchairs.*

Very little remains of Louis XIV's forest retreat of Marly but what does is hauntingly beautiful. The long vista from the *abreuvoir* (a large pool for watering horses) rises up through the now-bare terraces to the trees on the skyline. The château, the guest pavilions that were meant to represent signs of the zodiac, the sculptures, have all gone, but the sense of peace and seclusion that drew Louis to Marly still remains, even though the area is now a large public park.

As soon as Louis had had Versailles enlarged to his demands he looked about for somewhere else to escape from the noise and crowds and where he could entertain some of his favoured courtiers more privately and he decided on the site at Marly. What had been envisaged as a simple country retreat eventually became a very elaborate palace, with a splendid garden, a great cascade known as La Rivière, porcelain lined fishponds and a switchback railway. It soon became a matter of great concern to the courtiers whether or not they would be invited to the four-day 'retreats' at Marly and Louis would keep everyone on tenterhooks for as long as possible, by only issuing invitations at the last minute. It was the place where the king relaxed, bread rolls would be thrown during meals, there were gambling, picnics and concerts and the atmosphere was much freer than that at Versailles.

After Louis' death, Marly was shut up for economic reasons and allowed to fall into disrepair. It was briefly saved from being dismantled during the Regency when the cascade was removed, but it was finally demolished during the First Empire. It has been restored so that the broad outline of the site can be seen.

The site is horseshoe shaped, with the château sited at the closed end and with a splendid view over Paris from the other. There is a small museum showing what life was like at Marly on the N186 road, at the top of the park. It is possible to drive through the park and see the view and the site from the top, then drive down the road on either side of the park to the *abreuvoir* and look up the valley from below.

RAMBOUILLET
78120 Rambouillet. Tel: 34 83 21 21 (Office de Tourisme)

*50 km west of Paris on the N10 to Chartres.(53 E1)* **Opening hours:** *All year, 8 until sunset, except when the President is in residence. The dairy and the shell cottage are open every day except Tuesday, 10-12 and 2-6 (2-4 in winter).* **E.** *Free. Dairy very moderate in season and inexpensive out of season. Wheelchairs, (may be difficult in places, because of cobbles and gravel).*

The park at Rambouillet covers a large area to the south of the great château which was once Louis XVI's hunting lodge but is now a presidential residence. Immediately in front of the château are flower beds and a large water garden, a series of canals and geometric islands planted with trees. All these are on an extensive scale and were laid out in 1699 with the assistance of Le Nôtre.

The Comte de Toulouse, one of the bastard sons of Louis XIV bought Rambouillet and requested later that he be buried there 'like a pauper'. He was the only one of Louis's bastards who retained the respect of the court, according to St Simon. His son, the Duke of Penthièvre, was also a respected and virtuous man who remained safe during the Revolution because the people loved him. However, his son, the Prince de Lamballe, did not carry on the family tradition and died of debauchery at the age of 20. His young widow, a companion of Marie-Antoinette, died horribly in the Revolution. It had been for her, earlier, that the Duke of Penthièvre had made the *jardin anglais*. It is particularly pleasant with its winding rivulets, rocky waterfalls that enhance the sound of rushing water and rough stone bridge. At one end is a grotto with a statue above it.

Louis XVI, who wanted the hunting facilities of the forest of Rambouillet, acquired the château in 1783. When Marie Antoinette reputedly inquired: 'What am I to do in this Gothic toad hole?', Louis had a dairy constructed for her amusement. The queen's dairy was one of the last garden pavilions to be built before the Revolution. In style it resembles a severe classical temple. The first room is in marble, and then there is a cold room, the Salle de Refraichissement, where the milk was cooled. Water trickles down a grotto, round the statue La Chevrière, through ferns and ivy.

The other building to see is the Chaumière de Coquillages, the exquisite little Shell Cottage. It contains one room completely covered with a variety of sea shells and another elegantly painted with birds and flowers.

## ST GERMAIN-EN-LAYE
78103 St Germain-en-Laye

*20 km west of Paris on the N13 to Mantes-la-Jolie. The château is in the centre of the town.* **Opening hours:** *Every day 8-sunset. E. Free. Wheelchairs.*

The most exciting part of the garden is the Great Terrace, designed by Le Nôtre. Urns on the balustrade and a statue punctuate the view of the 3 km long terrace which ends at the Rond-Point de la Grille Royale. The limes that edge the walk were planted in 1745 and there is a splendid view over the river Seine.

The château, with its Le Nôtre *parterres*, is very much in the centre of the town - indeed, the tree-lined road leading out of the town is a continuation of the axis of the *parterres*. Between this building, the old château, and the Seine, was the new château, Châteauneuf, completed during the reign of Henri IV. One of the pavilions still remains and is now an expensive hotel. Below were terraces descending to the Seine and although the gardens have long since disappeared the steps remain. From these steps it is possible to glimpse the Pavillon du Sully (now a private residence) which used to be the Pavillon du Jardinier or gardener's house in what was the Jardin en

Dentelles of the new château. This still contains *parterres en broderie* in excellent condition.

The château at St Germain has many English connections. Mary Queen of Scots lived there for 12 years as did Charles II's sister, Henrietta, who was the first wife of the Duke of Orleans, brother to Louis XIV. James II, a very discontented exile, also lived at St Germain, from his deposition in 1688 to his death in 1701.

There is a tiny kiosk for tea and coffee, a bandstand and pony rides.

MUSEE DU PRIEURE
2 bis Rue Maurice Denis, 78100 St Germain-en-Laye. Tel: 39 73 77 87.

*South west of the château. The Rue au Pain by the information office leads directly to the Musée. **Opening hours:** Wednesday to Friday, 10-5.30; Saturday, Sunday and holidays, 10-6.30. E. Free to garden. Wheelchairs. Toilets. Salon du Thé.*

The priory was built in 1678 by Mme de Montespan as a hospital for the poor. It had been a Jesuit retreat for some years when the painter Maurice Denis acquired it in 1914. It is now a museum and gallery filled with paintings by Maurice Denis and his circle, the Nabis or Prophets, who were influenced by Japanese art and by the early Gauguin.

The garden is a peaceful 1 ha park that descends in flowery terraces. It contains statues, including Penelope waiting for Ulysses by J. Bourdelle, a rose pergola with graceful climbing roses, underplanted with geraniums and day lilies, and an orchard growing plums, pears, mirabelles and apples, planted as much for their blossom as for their fruit. It will, when the restoration is complete, have a yew-enclosed *solitude* and a *potager bouquetière*, a garden for growing flowers for cutting and a medicinal garden sited among the existing mature trees.

Also in the garden is an elegant Salon de Thé and a chapel, with murals by Maurice Denis.

VERSAILLES
78000 Versailles. Tel: 30 84 74 00.

*22 km west of Paris. The château is the centre of the town with three axes leading directly to it and to the statue of the Sun King in the forecourt.(35 E4). **Opening hours:** Gardens every day from sun rise to sunset, (Château closed on Mondays). E. Free for pedestrians. Entry when the fountains play (every Sunday from 3 May to 4 October at 11.15 and 3.30) inexpensive. Bicycles are very useful to cover the great area of the gardens and can be hired locally. Wheelchairs (and for hire). Toilet facilities in château and at the Trianons. Although the château is closed on Mondays and holidays, as are the Trianons - and that includes toilets - there is a* *toilet, including one for the disabled, open near the Trianons during part of Monday. Refreshments at the Palace and restaurant near the Trianons.*

In spite of the lack of facilities on a Monday, it is a very good day to visit the gardens as they are relatively quiet. There will still be enough people around to give the proper sense of scale to the breathtaking formal vista with its symmetry of pools, fountains, trees and statues, but not so many as to distract.

When Louis XIV had Versailles and its gardens built, he wanted a palace that would awe and dominate his court and his subjects by its magnificence. In a flat and unexciting terrain Andre Le Nôtre created just such a garden and its grandeur is still overwhelming today. The great canal in the shape of a cross and five miles round seems to recede into the distance beyond the immaculate *tapis vert* or green carpet of lawn laid between towering trees.

Immediately outside the palace are the Parterres d'Eau, two large pools adorned with statues symbolising the rivers Garonne and Loiret. The terrace forms part of a cross-axis. To the north the Parterres du Nord lead to the Allée d'Eau with its two rows of fountains falling into bowls held up sculptures of children and then to the circular Dragon Pool and Neptune Basin. To the south the Parterres du Midi overlook the magnificent orangery with its flanking stairways. From the same balustrade can be seen the Pièce d'Eau des Suisses, a large lake south of the St Cyr road. Regiments of Swiss soldiers were used to dig out the soil which was being used to raise the level in the new Potager du Roi. Unfortunately marsh gas released by the excavations killed many of the workers and Mme de Sevigné recorded that cartloads of dead bodies were removed every night.

Returning to the main axis, a large horseshoe terrace with ramps at either side leads down to the Bassin de Latone. Beyond the gently sloping *tapis vert* bordered with statues and urns - in winter, the statues are mysteriously shrouded and resemble headless monks - is the Basin of Apollo with a powerful statue of Apollo and his horses rising from the water.

Concealed among the trees on either side are smaller *bosquets* with pools, fountains, a colonnade, an obelisk and statues representing the four seasons. Like the statues of Latona and Apollo, many of the pieces of sculpture are symbolic tributes to Louis XIV.

It is possible to drive or cycle to the Trianons, but to walk along the *tapis vert* and by the edge of the canal, (where boats can be hired), is to properly experience the dimensions of the gardens and the gradual diminution of formality and scale.

The single-storied, colonnaded, pink marble **Grand Trianon** with its formal layout and slim cones of clipped yew, seems positively homely in contrast to the sheet of water of the Grand Canal. Louis XIV had demanded that this garden be full of flowers whenever he was there and this meant enormous labours of bedding out all year round. In 1672 10,000 tuberoses were brought up from Avignon and the gardener had to keep in readiness nearly two million flower pots. There is still bedding out in front of the Grand Trianon but on an exceedingly reduced scale.

The **Petit Trianon**, a perfect cube of soft golden stone presides over an even smaller garden, with clipped limes and walks leading to the unusually shaped Pavilion, the Salon de Musique. The rest of this garden is a miniature landscape of winding paths, meandering streams, rocky mounds and grottoes, a Claudian setting for a classical Temple of Love.

From there it is possible to walk through the landscape to the **Hameau,** that miniature village of beamed and thatched cottages, with a tower and a water mill, where Marie Antoinette played at being a peasant

Walking back to the palace from the *hameau*, do not fail to make a detour to the Neptune and Dragon fountains. Even when not functioning the Dragon Fountain is exciting with leaping fish and hissing swans being ridden by cherubs firing arrows at each other.

The **Potager du Roi**, the royal vegetable garden at 6 Rue Hardy is open from Wednesday to Sunday at 2.30 for a guided tour of 1 hour 30 minutes. (**E.** Moderate). The 9 ha garden and greenhouses with melons, pineapples, figs, peaches, apricots and trained pear trees, designed by Jean Baptiste La Quintinye the head gardener of Louis XIV, has been conserved in its original form. Fruit and vegetables are sold between 8.30 and 11.30 each Tuesday and Friday.

PARC BALBI
12 Rue du Marèchal Joffre, 78000 Versailles.

*Part of the Ecole Nationale Superieure d'Horticulture et du Paysage. Facing the château, turn left down the Rue Independence Americain, left into Rue de l'Orangerie and right into Rue du Marèchal Joffre. Opening hours: Every day except Mondays and holidays. 1 April to 30 September 1-6; 1 October to 31 March 1-5. E. Free. Wheelchairs.*

The garden of Madame Balbi is a tree and shrub garden, with winding streams and a serpentine lake, designed for walking around and enjoying nature. Unfortunately the authorities have fenced off the grotto and the belvedere that stand at one end of the small lake. Not only is this visually very obtrusive but it prevents a proper perambulation of the garden, which was part of its original charm and purpose, although the grotto can be visited as part of a visit to the Potager du Roi, above.

# CENTRAL FRANCE

## AUVERGNE

**ALLIER**

PARC D'ALLIER
Boulevard Prèsident John Kennedy, 03200 Vichy.

*Coming into Vichy from Clermont Ferrand, turn left after crossing the Pont de Bellerive across the lac d'Allier. (100 B4) **Opening hours:** Every day, permanently. E. Free. Wheelchairs. Toilets. Guided visits once a week in summer*

The municipal Parc d'Allier is a long and narrow promenade by the river Allier. It was designed around 1852 for the Emperor Napoleon III and was planted with unusual trees.

As well as the trees, which include *Cladrastis lutea* (yellow-wood) from America, a magnificent weeping beech, and a *Maclura pomifera*, the Osage orange, there are bedding plants, old roses and a pond with a fountain surrounded by irises, acanthus and hemerocallis.

This is a pleasant place for a stroll if you are in Vichy but hardly worth a special journey.

## LA BALAINE
03460 Villeneuve-sur-Allier. Tel: 70 43 30 07.

*Leave Villeneuve-sur-Allier on the N7 towards Nevers and take the first right turn on to the D433. The arboretum is signed. (86 A4)* **Opening hours:** *April to November, every day 10-12 and 2-7.* **E.** *Moderate. Wheelchairs, access to much of the grounds. Toilets. Refreshments.*

Although Balaine is an arboretum, and is in fact the oldest privately owned arboretum in France, it contains much more than the name suggests. It is a woodland garden like Wakehurst Place or Bodnant and the trees are underplanted with rhododendrons, azaleas, bamboos, cytisus and hydrangea species.

The garden was created at the beginning of the nineteenth century by Aglaé Adanson, the daughter of a celebrated botanist and philosopher, Michel Adanson, and it has been continually added to by subsequent owners. There are collections of maples and of bamboos as well as a fine *Sophora japonica* 'pendula' and a good specimen of the shrubby June-flowering *Lonicera quinquelocularis* and a dramatic *Picea orientalis* 'Aurea repens'.

By the entrance is a pretty meadow and nearer the château with its moat, are large herbaceous borders edged with sedums and houseleeks. A glasshouse contains a collection of cacti and there is an interesting nursery selling some very desirable plants. There are 1,200 different tree species and shrubs spread over 20 ha of woodland, winding streams, and lakes, a picturesque setting for a magnificent collection of plants.

## PUY DE DOME

## LA BATISSE
63450 Chanonat. Tel: 70 79 41 04.

*12 km south of Clermont Ferrand. Leave by N9 to Issoire and after 9 km take the turning to Chanonat to the west. La Bâtisse is 1 km through the village and on the left. (113 D2).* **Opening hours:** *1 July to 31 August, every day, 10-12 and 2-7; 1 April to 30 June and 1 September to 31 October, every day except Tuesday, 2.30-6.* **E.** *Inexpensive. Toilets.*

In front of the building are three pools with fountains, a formal arrangement, said to have been designed by André le Nôtre. A double staircase leads to a lower *parterre* with a circular central pool and flower borders with irises and peonies. Two small pavilions stand at the corners of the garden by the edge of the river. Across the river is an arrangement of bushes, *Acer campestre* and others, described as a labyrinth. Further along, framed by an avenue of sycamores and other trees, is an exciting cascade.

JARDIN DES CROISADES, CHATEAU DE BUSSEOL
63270 Vic-le-Comte. Tel: 73 69 00 84.

*South east of Clermont Ferrand on the N9 to Vic-le-Comte and Issoire. Turn left onto the D212 to Billom on the edge of the city and then take the D1 at Perignat-sur-Allier. After about 4 km, fork left to Busséol, bypassing the village of Mirefleurs. (113 E2)* **Opening hours:** *Every day from 15 June to 15 September, 10-12 and 2-6; Sundays and holidays 1 March to 14 June and 16 September to 11 November, 2.30-5.30. Guided visits only but not much time in the garden. E. Moderate.*

The twelfth century castle of Busséol stands proudly on a hill overlooking the beautiful countryside of the Auvergne. The very compact gardens which are entirely within the walls are a recreation of a mediaeval garden, using indigenous native plants and mediterranean plants that were introduced in the Middle Ages.

This is not a visit for the infirm or elderly as there is a stiff climb from the car park up to the fortified castle.

CHATEAU DE CORDES
63210 Orcival. Tel: 73 65 81 34.

*South-west of Clermont Ferrand, about 26 km either by D941A through Chamalières or N89 towards Mont Dore and La Bourboule. At the crossroads where the N89 meets the D941A, take the minor road, the D216 south to Orcival. The road divides into three after 4 km. Take the centre road, still signed to Orcival and the entrance to Cordès is on the right. The château is at the end of a steep sided valley and there is a long drive through parkland. (139 E4)* **Opening hours:** *30 June to 2 September, every day 10-12 and 2-6. E. Moderate. Wheelchairs. Toilets.*

The garden at Cordès is noted for its Le Nôtre *parterres*. These famous *parterres* are hidden by 25 feet high double beech hedges which seem even higher as one walks down the sunken, narrow driveway. Only an aerial view really does the design justice.

The beech hedges extend to form a semi-circle round the *cour d'honneur*. Inside the court are two circular beds with ornamental pools and balls and cones of clipped box and yew. The château itself, unlike the garden, is entirely asymmetrical, with Sleeping Beauty towers at every corner. This garden will delight the Le Nôtre connoisseur not least for the contrast between its immaculately kept formality and the wild Auvergne setting.

EFFIAT
63260 Aigueperse. Tel: 73 63 64 01.

*On D984 south west of Vichy. Follow signs to Aigueperse and Riom.* **Opening hours:** *Liable to change. 1 March to 30 June and mid-September to end November, weekends and holidays, 3-7. Mid June to mid September, every day 9-12 and 2.30-7. Sunday, 10-12 and 3-7. Guided visits. Illuminated visits certain evenings in July and August.(100 A4).* **E.** *Moderate. Toilets. Wheelchairs.*

Unfortunately I did not succeed in visiting this garden as the owner did not keep to his own opening dates so it is not possible to describe the garden fully or to recommend a detour to visit it. The opening times given above are exactly as the owner has said but it might be wise to telephone first.

The garden is said to have been designed by André Mollet, one of a dynasty of French gardeners, who worked in England at St James's Palace and Wimbledon House in the middle of the seventeenth century. It is said to contain a long terrace, canals with bridges, a *nymphée* or grotto, pavilions, topiary and *parterres a l'anglaise* plus roses, water lilies and amaryllis. Access is through a handsome triumphal arch at the end of an avenue of limes leading from the village.

# BURGUNDY    FRANCHE-COMTÉ

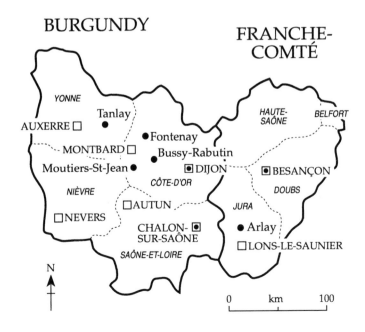

# BURGUNDY

## COTE D'OR

ABBAYE DE FONTENAY
21500 Montbard. Tel: 80 92 15 00. Fax: 80 92 16 88.

*6 km from Montbard. Turn off the D905 at Marmagne east of Montbard on to the D32. Well signed. (73 D2)* **Opening hours:** *Guided tours 15 March to 15 November, every hour (July and August, every half hour) 9-12 and 2.30-6. 15 November to 15 March, 9-12 and 2-5 unguided. E. moderate. Toilets. Wheelchairs.*

This twelfth century Cistercian abbey, a World Heritage site, is idyllicly situated in the heart of the Forest of Fontenay, surrounded by springs and streams, smooth lawns and tranquil planting.

In the first courtyard a spring gushes up from a flat, circular millstone and huge plane and ash trees pattern the grass and gravel with shadows. To the right is a *château d'eau*, a curved, four-tiered waterfall. Water flows from a spring in a wall, spreads out like the layers of a crinoline skirt and falls into a rectangular pool. Behind the wall is a terrace ornamented with large terracotta pots and at the sides of the pool are borders of pink roses.

A few carefully chosen climbing plants and roses enhance the soft sandy stone of the monastery walls. At the back of the abbey buildings there is a well-proportioned *parterre,* with an enclosing ridge of trees on one side. A circular pond with a high rim collects the water from a spring that flows down a set of steps with a narrow cascade down the middle. A mixed border of roses, foliage plants, hemerocallis, peonies, lupins and hostas edged with a drift of rock roses has been planted at each side of this garden.

The way the monastic buildings relate to each other adds a sense of discovery to the gardens - only one area can be seen at a time. Some, like the cloister, have to be especially sought out. The planting, apart from the herbaceous border, is very simple: a row of pink hydrangeas or pink and blue hibiscus at the foot of a wall. A garden of monastic serenity.

BUSSY RABUTIN
Bussy Rabutin, 21150 Les Laumes. Tel: 80 96 00 03.

*Go south of Montbard on the D905 to Vitteaux. After 14 km turn east in Les Laumes on to the D954. Bussy-Rabutin is signed. (73 E3)* **Opening hours:** *Every day, 1 April to 30 September, 10-12 and 2-7. 1 October to 30 March, 10-12 and 2-4, Closed Tuesday and Wednesday. Closed 1 January, 1 May, 1 and 11 November and 25 December. Tours of the château on the hour. E. Moderate. Toilets. Wheelchairs.*

This château is sited so snugly in its valley that the gate to it comes as a surprise. It is a romantic setting, quite fit for the articulate and witty courtier, Roger de Rabutin, Comte de Bussy, who spent his last years decorating the château.

The count, who was also a cousin and correspondent of Mme de Sevigné, was exiled to his estates in 1665 after the publication of his scandalous account of life at the court of Louis XIV. During his 16 years of exile he devoted himself to embellishing his château and its grounds. He rebuilt the bridge over the moat and added pediments, pilasters, niches and dormer windows to the centre façade.

The *cour d'honneur* of the château faces the closed end of the valley, sheltered by woods and ornamented with a statue of the Rape of Proserpine. Mysterious flights of steps recede into the trees. Another statue stands, unreachable, high above.

The other side of the château looks down to the village and out of the valley, over a formal garden with four lawns edged with espaliered apple trees and clipped box. The apple trees are interspersed with herbaceous plants, peonies and michaelmas daisies. Water gushes out from a fountain and crosses the garden in a small rill, feeding a central round pond, emptying under a balustrade into a rectangular pond and then to a small lake in the valley below. A gravel terrace has statues at either end and two central ornaments, sixteenth century campanile taken from a house in Dijon, that echo the two towers of the garden front of the château.

JARDIN DE L'ARQUEBUSE
1 Avenue Albert 1er, 21033 Dijon.

*Opposite the railway station on the N5 from Montbard. Keep right, on the park's perimeter, to find a parking place. (74 B4)* **Opening hours:** *Every day; summer, 7.30am-8pm; winter, 7.30-5.30. E. Free. Wheelchairs. Toilets.*

The Jardin de l'Arquebuse contains more than just the botanic garden: statues, a rotunda, small temples of love and a wooded area with a *boules* pitch, lake and small river, complete the site.

However it is the botanic garden, founded in 1883, that will be of most interest to the garden enthusiast. It contains well-kept and extensive order beds, the outer ones edged with colorful bedding plants, arranged symmetrically about a central pool and fountain. There are good collections of grasses, ferns, irises, dianthus and campanulas. The collection of solanums is interesting, containing the original species from which tomatoes, peppers and other vegetables are derived, including *Cyphomandra betacea* and *Solanum pyracanthum* with long orange thorns. Each area is well documented.

In the wooded area are a *Sophora japonica*, a 12 foot high *Amorpha fruticosa*, a *Torreya nucifera*, as well as a giant cedar of Lebanon, a *Populus yunnanensis* and a *Fraxinus americana*, several enormous plane trees, oriental and the London plane, and a 150 year old *Toona ciliata (Cedrela chinensis)* a handsome ailanthus-like tree, but suffering somewhat from its age.

Plant lovers will find this garden interesting and enjoyable.

Also in Dijon is the **Parc de la Colombière** (From the town centre go to the great roundabout of the Place Wilson and drive down the magnificent Cours General de Gaulle to the south-east.) This park may have been planned by Le Nôtre, as is sometimes said, but the plans were carried out by his Dijon pupil, Antoine de Maerle. A square of woodland has radiating *allées* around an open central area - now a lawn with two beds of bedding plants. There are three main axes and some of the trees date from the inception of the garden. The *Temple d'amour* is a classified historic monument, as is the park itself making the site of interest to historians. Other visitors may find it rather dull.

JARDIN COEUR DE ROY
21500 Moutiers-Saint-Jean.

*Take the D980 south-east of Montbard to Saulieu. Just outside Montbard turn right to Crepand, then go through the villages of St Germain, Senailly and Athie to Moutiers St-Jean. Continue to the top of Moutiers St-Jean and turn left just after the church. (73 D3).* **Opening hours:** *4-5 June,1 July or 31 August, 12-6. (The garden can be seen from the road)* **E.** *Free.*

For garden historians and anyone who likes to discover unknown France, this walled garden is intriguing. Elaborate arches pierce the walls. It is possible to look through a wrought iron grille to a grassy terrace with stone obelisks, and down to a lower level. To the right is the round roof of a sunken building and to the left an imposing wall with a niche, and pediments and decorative balls. There are fruit trees trained round the walls and rose bushes here and there.

Another glance over the wall further down reveals that the round roof covers a small pavilion, cut right into a bank between two levels of garden and that it has an elaborate entrance. It was not until the appearance of 'The Secret Gardens of France' by Mirabel Osler that I was able to discover more about this mysterious garden. It was made after 1683 by Jean Coeur-de-Roy, President of the *parlement* at Dijon, whose family home Moutiers-St-Jean was. Originally there were eight gateways and the fishponds and fountains were the envy of the Auxois. An old photograph has revealed the existence of a pond in the centre and there are plans to restore it in the future. Now only the merest vestiges of that grand garden remain, but it is still hauntingly beautiful.

## SAONE ET LOIRE

### JARDIN BOTANIQUE, CHALON-SUR-SAONE
Parc Georges Nouelle, 71100 Chalon-sur-Saône.

*Part of the public park, Parc Georges Nouelle, which is to the east of the town where the road by the river Saône turns left away from the river and towards Verdun-sur-le-Doubs. (88 A3)* **Opening hours:** *Every day. E. Free. Wheelchairs.*

This small botanic section of a larger public park is well worth visiting if you are in the town. A large rockery area has rock and herbaceous plants, well (but not always correctly) labelled. Another rocky part is planted interestingly with ferns and grasses. *Panicum virgatum* with purplish panicles and introduced to Europe from America in 1781, is one of the many grasses that are used well in this garden.

There are two ponds, one with ducks and a grotto, the other planted with marginal plants, rushes and grasses. An unusual and very successful feature is the large area planted with varieties of hemerocallis.

Also in Chalon is the **Roseraie Saint-Nicholas,** 4 km to the east. Take the bridge Pont St Laurent and cross the two islands, then turn left in Rue Julien Leneuvreu. Open from early June to early October. As well as an International Concours des Roses, there is a rockery, arboretum, water garden and heather garden.

## YONNE

### TANLAY
89430 Tanlay. Tel 86 75 70 61.

*East of Tonnerre, on the D965 to Châtillon-sur-Seine. Well signed in Tanlay. (72 C1). Open Easter to All Saints, every day except Tuesday. Guided tours of the château at 9.30, 10.30, 11.30 and 2.15, 3, 3.45, 4.30 and 5.15. E. Moderate. Wheelchairs. Toilets (basic) outside grounds.*

An imposing double avenue of elms leads from the town to the main gates of the château, and the vista continues to the inner arch of the Petit Château across a grassed courtyard surrounded by the stables. Another gateway opposite leads to the park. Inhabitants of the town walk in the park but visitors tend to be shepherded towards the château for the tours.

The château, one of the most important in Burgundy, was completed by architect Philippe de Muet in the mid-seventeenth century and is a good example of French Renaissance architecture. It is at right angles to the long vista and is surrounded by a moat. The moat bridge is guarded by two sentry boxes topped with obelisks. On the other side is an attractive gatehouse, also by Le Muet. Beyond the bridge is the *cour d'honneur* of the Grand Château.

The most interesting part of the garden for the historian is the 526m long canal that feeds the moat. An imposing *château d'eau*, a rusticated screen, disguises the pond in which the waters are collected. The canal is actually narrowed to increase the illusion of length.

## CENTRE

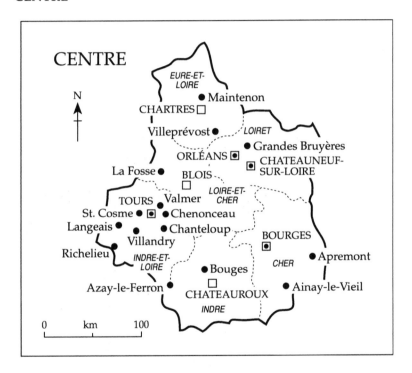

## CHER

CHATEAU D'AINAY-LE-VIEIL
18200 Saint-Amand-Montrond. Tel: 48 63 50 67.

*South of Bourges on the N144, towards Montluçon and 10 km south of St-Amand, take the D1 west. (85 D4). Opening hours: Roseraie, June and September, 10-12 and 2-7; July and August 10-7. Château, 5 February to 30 November, same hours. E. Gardens, inexpensive; château and gardens, moderate. Toilets, nearby in village.*

The fortified château, a Renaissance building protected by high walls and nine circular towers with conical roofs, and surrounded by a moat with running water, is set in an English style park. It is a romantic sight especially when seen through the flower laden arches of one of the rose gardens. As well as a landscaped rose garden with modern roses, 200 varieties of old and species roses dating from the fifteenth century are planted in related groups and underplanted with bulbs. There are also topiary replicas of two Renaissance pavilions which frame an ornamental pond.

Parc Floral d'Apremont

PARC FLORAL D'APREMONT
18150 La Guerche-sur-L'Aubois. Tel: 48 80 41 41.

*Take the N7 out of Nevers to Bourges and Moulins and then, after 3.5 km, the D976 to Bourges. After about 7 km the road crosses the river Allier and the turning to Apremont-sur-Allier, to the south, is signed. (85 F3)* **Opening hours:** *Sunday before Easter to mid-September every day, except Tuesday, 10-12 and 2-7. From 1 June, open on Tuesday afternoon. E. Moderate. Wheelchairs. Toilets. Restaurant.*

The Parc Floral is the showpiece of a restored mediaeval village situated behind and between the pretty stone cottages which are each liberally planted with flowers and climbers. The park was started in 1971 by Gilles de Brissac as a public exhibition garden to show a wide variety of well-grown plants. Indeed, the first sight as one enters in early summer is of cottage walls heavy with large flowered clematis.

There is a white border, based on the famous white garden at Sissinghurst and a large summer border, planted with lupins, shrub roses, geraniums, mulleins, columbines, artemisias, salvias, foxgloves and, for foliage effect, cardoons, rue and a variety of grasses. Near the summer border is a spectacular pergola, dazzling with the hanging flowers of laburnum, white and blue wisteria and pink robinia.

An upper valley has been dammed to provide a series of ponds, separated by waterfalls and crossed by a red Chinese bridge. The margins are planted with iris, alchemilla, junipers and marginal plants. The series of three lakes behind are bordered with roses 'Roseraie de l'Hay' and 'Le Cid' and *Salix elaeagnos angustifolia*. In the ponds water lilies and lotus flourish. As well as the summer border, there is a spring border, a rock garden and good collections of conifers and deciduous trees.

PRES FICHAUX
Boulevard de la République, 18000 Bourges.

*North of the town centre, just before the Carrefour de Verdun between the inner and outer ring roads. (84 C2)* **Opening hours:** *Every day 7.30-sunset. E. Free. Wheelchairs. Toilets, basic. Café.*

The entrance to this public park does not do justice to the imaginative design of the park itself. The Prés Fichaux was laid out by landscape architect Paul Marguerita in 1922 and has been described as 'an interesting modern variation of the traditional regular style'.

Immediately beyond the entrance is the *théâtre de verdure* or open air theatre created from green hedges. Rows of pleached limes and new plantings of camellias lead to the rest of the park. Trimmed cones of *Magnolia grandiflora* and triangular beds edged with *Lonicera nitida* and filled with the pink, white and green leaves of *Acer negundo* have a freshness and originality unusual in a public park, but the most striking features are the long, crisp lines of linked yew arches and the rose globes. Roses are trained round spherical iron frames and when they are in bloom form spectacular orbs of leaf and flower. Two rectangular pools reflect their attendant statues among the water lilies.

Also in Bourges visit the **Jardins de l'Archevêché** (Rue des Hémerettes, near the cathedral, open all the time). The garden is divided into two parts: a shady area with children's play equipment, a *bassin*, a fountain and a formal area with beds divided by lines of pleached limes. The design of the garden is believed to be by Pitron, a contemporary of Le Nôtre. It is very well maintained.

## EURE ET LOIR

√ MAINTENON
28130 Maintenon. Tel: 37 23 00 09.

*Maintenon is north of Chartres via the D906 or use the prettier D6. The château is on the right just over the river when entering the town. (53 D1)* **Opening hours:** *1 April to 31 October, every day except Tuesday, 2-6.30. Sundays and holidays, 10-12 and 2-6.30. 1 November to 31 March, Saturday and Sunday 2-5. Closed from 17 December and for January. E. Château, moderate. Wheelchairs, possible as far as parterre. Toilets.*

The château and garden are surrounded by the rivers Eure and Voise which are joined to form a moat and a canal. The main *parterre* is very simple being of grass with an edging and central motif in crushed brick. The garden, small and quickly seen, was redesigned by Le Nôtre in 1676 for Mme de Maintenon. This powerful and often unpopular woman was first of all, governess to the children of Mme de Montespan, Louis XIV's mistress, then mistress herself to Louis and, finally, his wife.

The surrounding park is being turned into a golf course and this has caused the water level of the moat to fall and reduced the attractiveness of the setting. In the distance, at the end of the canal, are the ruins of the great aqueduct that was part of a grandiose scheme to carry the waters of the Eure to Versailles. Several workmen were killed during its construction, costs mounted alarmingly and it was never finished. It is not possible to walk from the garden to the aqueduct but it is a romantic if melancholy sight with trees and bushes growing from its crumbling stones.

VILLEPREVOST
28140 Orgères-en-Beauce. Tel: 37 99 45 17.

*40 km south-east of Chartres via the N154 to Orleans. Turn right at Allaines on to the D927 to Orgères-en-Beauce. After about 9 km, turn left to village of Villeprévost. (53 E3)* **Opening hours:** *15 April to 15 October, weekends and holidays 2-6.30. E. Moderate. Wheelchairs possible. Toilets.*

Designed in 1756 by one of the gardeners from Versailles after the precepts of Le Nôtre, Villeprévost is a classic park of the eighteenth century. It covers 10 ha and is enclosed by walls. Unusually it is designed on an axis that is based on the position in which the sun sets on 15 August, in honour of the chatelain of that time whose fête day it was. Apparently the Grand Canal at Versailles was orientated in the same way: the relevant date there is 25 August, Louis XIV's saint's day.

The garden was neglected during the nineteenth century but was restored under the instructions of the present owner's grandfather, by a landscape architect from Orleans.

The main axis is bordered by clipped hornbeams and embellished with urns. Trimmed yews and narrow flower beds lead from the entrance arch to the typical eighteenth century Beauce manor house.

## INDRE

AZAY-LE-FERRON
36290 Azay-le-Ferron. Tel: 54 39 20 06.

*In the centre of the village which is 17 km south-west of Châtillon-sur-Indre on the D975 signed to Le Blanc and 33 km due south of Loches. (82 C3)* **Opening hours:** *1 April to 30 September, every day except Tuesday, 10-12 and 2-6. October and March, Wednesday, Saturday, Sunday and holidays 10-12 and 2-5. November, December and February, 10-12 and 2-4.30 on the same days. Closed on 1 and 11 November, 25 December and throughout January. E. Inexpensive. Wheelchairs.*

One of the last members of the family that had owned the château since 1852 left it to the town of Tours in 1951. The château, like the garden, is a mixture of styles. In front of the main façade is a box *parterre,* a *boulingrin* and an important feature of the garden is the much photographed and very striking topiary of box and yew. Outside the orangery is a formal flower garden, with a central pool and magnolias. The whole is surrounded by an English style landscape park, made with the help of the Bühler brothers between 1856-1872, with fine specimen trees. They include an oak dating from about 1650, limes, liquidambars, Atlas cedars and hornbeams.

## CHATEAU DE BOUGES
Bouges-le-Château, 36110 Levroux. Tel: 54 35 88 26.

*18 km south of Valençay and 30 km north of Châteauroux. From Valençay take the D956 and turn left on to the D34 to Rouvres-les-Bois. After the village take the D37 to Bouges-le-Château. From Châteauroux take the D956 and turn right to Bouges just beyond the village of Levroux. (83 F2)* **Opening hours:** *1 April to 30 June every day except Tuesday 10-12 and 2-6 (7 in June); 1 July to 31 August, every day 10-1 and 2-7; September and October, every day except Tuesday, 10-12 and 2-5. November and March, Saturday and Sunday 2-5. Closed in December, January and February. E. Very moderate.. Wheelchairs. Toilets.*

The elegant small château, a cube of honey colored stone like the Petit Trianon, has a fine *parterre en broderie* of grass and clipped box surrounded by a balustrade. *Allées* of lime trees, topiary yew, avenues of plane and chestnut, all increase the sense of harmony and order.

Beyond the formal garden is an extensive *parc a l'anglaise* with many different tree species that are particularly fine in autumn and an attractive lake. Beyond the *cour des communs* or courtyard of the outbuildings is a small flower garden inspired by mediaeval designs, bright with dahlias in late summer. There are also greenhouses.


## INDRE ET LOIRE

PAGODE DE CHANTELOUP
37400 Amboise. Tel: 47 57 90 97. Fax: 47 57 65 90.

*2 km south of Amboise.. Take the D31 to Bléré.. Well signed. (68 A4)* **Opening hours:** *Every day; from mid-February 10-12 and 2-5; March to 5.30, April to 6. May, 10-6; June, 10-7; July and August, 9.30-8; September 10-7; October,10-1 and 2-6 (5 to mid November) E. Moderate. Wheelchairs. Picnic meals available.*

The pagoda is the only remaining artefact from the gardens of the Château de Chanteloup, an estate belonging to the Duke of Choiseul, one of Louis XV's ministers. When the duke was dismissed from the king's service, he dedicated the pagoda to friendship as a sign of gratitude to those friends who remained faithful.

The pagoda was built between 1775 and 1778 and its design is based on Sir William Chambers' celebrated Chinese Pagoda at Kew. It was once part of an immense vista and some of the *allées* that were part of the garden can be glimpsed in the marshy forest of Amboise. The pagoda stands by a pool edged with reeds, in a slightly melancholy landscape: a strange mixture of classical eighteenth century French architecture and chinoiserie to see in such a site. It is possible to climb the tower.

## CHENONCEAU
37150 Chenonceaux. Tel: 47 23 90 07.

*10 1/2 km south of Amboise via the D81 or 25 km east of Tours on N76, then east to Bléré by the D40.(68 A4). **Opening hours:** Every day. 16 March to 15 September, 9-7; 16 to 30 September, 9-6.30; October, 9-6; 1 to 15 November, 9-5; 16 November to 15 February, 9-12 and 2-4.30; 16 to 28 February, 9-5.30; 1 to 15 March, 9-6. E. Moderate. Wheelchairs. Toilets. Tea room and snack bar.*

Try to visit Chenonceau out of season if possible - it is a famous tourist attraction and can be overwhelmed by visitors in July and August.

A fine avenue of plane trees leads towards the courtyard on which stood the original mediaeval castle surrounded by a moat. The château is beyond that, rising out of the waters of the river Cher. The Italian gardens of Diane de Poitiers are on the left and those of Catherine de Medici are on the right. Henry II gave Chenonceau to his mistress Diane de Poitiers and it was she who initially built the graceful five-arched bridge over the river Cher, to a design by Philibert De l'Orme, one of the architects of the Palace of Fontainebleau. When Henry died, his widow, Catherine de Medici, made Diane leave and took over Chenonceau herself. She was responsible for having the great park laid out and the two storey extension built over the bridge. The first level of this is now one long gallery.

The two *parterres* are both formal designs, with scrolls, domes of clipped evergreens and central pools. Catherine de Medici's garden is the site of the former Fontaine du Rocher where she held some lavish entertainments.

## LANGEAIS
37130 Langeais. Tel: 47 96 72 60. Fax: 47 96 54 44.

*In the centre of the town of Langeais which is on the banks of the Loire west of Tours. Take the N152 on the north bank of the river. (67 E4) **Opening hours:** Every day, 15 March to 15 July and 1 September to 2 November, 9-6.30; 16 July to 31 August, 9am - 10pm; 3 November to 14 March, 9-12 and 2-5. E. Moderate. Toilets.*

The tiny garden beyond the courtyard at Langeais is a reconstruction of a fifteenth century garden. The marriage of Charles VIII of France and Anne of Brittany, who were both enthusiastic gardeners, was celebrated there in 1491.

The garden is a small formal *parterre* edged with trellis and with domes of clipped euonymus. Low walls are topped with grass to make seats. There are little motifs of clipped box and a central fountain protected by walls of trimmed yew resembling the backgrounds of mediaeval French paintings. The garden is overlooked by the ruins of the oldest keep still in existence in France built towards the end of the tenth century by the Count of Anjou.

PARC RICHELIEU
Place du Cardinal de Richelieu, 37120 Richelieu.

*21 km south of Chinon on the D749. The entrance to the park is on the D749.(81 F2) Opening hours: 15 June to 15 September, 10-6.30. E. Inexpensive. Toilets. Wheelchairs.*

Cardinal Richelieu bought the village and manor of Richelieu very early in his career and destroyed many neighbouring châteaux in his efforts to make Richelieu the only important building for miles around. Little now remains of his grandiose project, although the adjoining town of Richelieu is still worth seeing: a complete seventeenth century 'planned' town on a grid system, surrounded by a wall.

The château has disappeared but some of the formal gardens, and several of the smaller buildings can be found, including the domed lodge, two pavilions, an orangery and wine cellars. Canals and straight avenues of chestnut and plane trees give some indication of the original design.

PRIEURE ST-COSME
37520 La Riche. Tel: 47 37 32 70.

*The priory is situated on the banks of the Loire, 3 kms west of Tours in the suburb of La Riche. From the centre of Tours, drive towards the river and then take the Avenue Proudhon along the south bank to the west. The priory is well signed. (67 F4) Opening hours: 15 March to 30 June, and September, every day, 9-12.30 and 1.30-6; July and August, 9-6; 1 October to 14 March, closed on Monday, 9-12.30 and 1.30-5. Closed December and January. E. Moderate. Wheelchairs. Toilets.*

The sixteenth century poet Pierre Ronsard became prior at St-Cosme in 1564 and died there in 1585. The priory was bombed in 1944 but has been recently restored and ten different garden areas have been created around the buildings and the ruins.

The designers seem to have taken a line of one of Ronsard's most famous poems, *Mignonne, allons voir si la Rose...* to heart and largely planted this new garden with roses though there are many irises too. They have, however, missed the opportunity to plant a sixteenth century garden using the 'purple-robed' gallicas that Ronsard refers to and it is the brighter, more indestructible modern roses that are used through the garden. Standard roses are underplanted with bush roses such as 'Bonica', 'Pascali' and 'Dearest'.

There is a *potager,* and a fruit garden, the Jardin des Velours, planted with trained apricot, apple and plum trees.

JARDIN BOTANIQUE, TOURS
Boulevard Tonnelé, 37000 Tours.

*South-west of town centre. At the west end of the Boulevard Beranger, the main, wide boulevard that cuts the town into north and south, turn left into Rue Girardeau and go as far as the Place Rabelais, turn right into Rue Plat d'Etain and the Jardin Botanique is signed. Go past the barracks and turn right at the junction. (67 F4)* **Opening hours:** *Every day 8.30-5.30.(The Jardin des Simples is open from 15 March to 15 November, Monday to Friday 2-6.)* **E.** *Free. Wheelchairs Toilets basic.*

As well as the glasshouses, the herb garden and plant order beds, this well-stocked botanic garden has a small zoo with birds and animals in cages. The arboretum contains some good trees, many over 100 years old and possibly dating from the garden's creation in 1843.

The order beds are set out according to Cronquist's classification of the evolution of vegetable families. A large board very usefully sets out what these are and how the plants relate to each other. In a particularly attractive area there are collections of irises, peonies, whole beds of phlox and a particularly good assortment of liliaceae: lilies, eremurus, alliums, fritillaries and crinums. Herbaceous plants grow in a border down one side of a central path bordered by tubs of clipped bougainvillea that separates the order beds from a heather garden, a rock bank, magnolias and clumps of rhododendrons on the other side. In the spring there is a display of flowering bulbs.

The Jardin des Simples, with its medicinal and poisonous plants, is wisely kept under supervision and is not open all the time. It is full of interesting scents - heavy, aromatic, sharp - and the plants are laid out in geometric, box edged beds. The subjects are divided into dyes, narcotics and plants for different medical uses.

Also in Tours is the **Jardin Prebendes d'Oe** in the Rue de Bois Denier (take the Avenue de Grammont, the main through road to Poitiers and after about half a kilometre turn right into Rue R. Salengro. Open all the time). Designed by the Bühler brothers in 1872, this public park is very typical of their style. There is a pleasant lake with water lilies and gunnera growing on the margin and good trees.

JARDINS DE VALMER
Chançay, 37210 Vouvray. Tel: 47 52 93 12. Fax: 47 52 26 92.

*The Château of Valmer is 15 km north east of Tours and 5 km north of Vouvray. On the A10 Paris-Tours autoroute, take the exit to Vouvray. (68 A4)* **Opening hours:** *1 July to 31 August, every day except Monday, 2.30-7.* **E.** *Gardens and chapel, moderate. Toilets.*

The Château of Valmer was destroyed by fire in 1948 but the seventeenth century Italianate terrace garden remains. The first terrace is called the Terrace of the Fountains, after the Florentine fountains there. The upper terrace has four squares of clipped hornbeam with a stone pillar, which came from the nearby château at Chanteloup when it was destroyed, supporting a vase in the centre. From one corner of this terrace there is a panoramic view of Valmer, the terraces, the valley of the river Brenne and the grand canal; from another viewpoint the fine avenue of chestnuts which mark the entrance drive and the vineyards can be seen. The château produces a fine Vouvray wine. The Leda Terrace has lost its statue of Leda to the Metropolitan museum in New York.

A vegetable garden, arranged in four squares around a central pond and edged with espalier pear trees, is being restored. The adjoining park has its original avenues marked with lines of hornbeams and punctuated with more columns from Chanteloup.

## VILLANDRY
Villandry, 37510 Joué-lès-Tours. Tel: 47 50 02 09.

*18 km west of Tours, on the D7 south of the river Loire. (67 E4)* **Opening hours:** *Every day 8.30 or 9-sunset* **E.** *Moderate. Wheelchairs. Toilets.*

Villandry with its ornamental vegetable garden, must be one of the handful of French gardens that is known, at least by name, to every gardener. And it must be said that its fame is well deserved - it is quite splendid both in its overall effect and in its detail.

The gardens at Villandry are a reconstruction of the formal gardens of the sixteenth century and as such, are unique in France. In the nineteenth century many formal French gardens were swept away in favour of the English landscape style. However, at the beginning of this century fashions changed again and there was a move back to the traditional French pattern of geometric layouts, box edging, vistas and *allées*. Dr Joachim Carvallo; bought Villandry in 1906 and round the renaissance château with its remaining eighteenth century canals and terraces, began the work of recreating a French *potager* and an ornamental garden, known as the Garden of Love. The work took him 18 years.

The gardens are on three levels and the main axis is the lime walk that separates the lower gardens from the earlier water garden.

The *potager* surrounded by espaliered apple and pear trees, is made up of nine squares each made up of different geometric designs outlined in box. The outer beds contain flowers but the inner ones are of vegetables, chosen for their leaf color and texture. Each of the nine squares has its central fountain, while the central square has rose arbours at each corner. The logistics of the planting are fascinating. There are two plantings a year and both are different every year. Crop rotation is also practiced! As well as all this, plants with leaves of a similar green have to be kept apart. It makes the problems of ordinary gardeners seem quite easy. The penetrating light green of lettuce, the blue green of cabbages, tall grey green broad beans, spikes of chives and leeks, the different reds of ruby chard and radiccio all combine to make richly colored patterns in the box-edged beds. Parsley adds its unique texture, while in the summer the vibrant colors of tomatoes, peppers and aubergines contribute to the splendour. Standard roses and pear trees give the *parterre* height.

On the far side of the *potager* is a recently planted herb garden, containing medicinal, aromatic and culinary herbs, 32 different species in all.

The ornamental garden is divided into two sections, both with outlines and patterns of tall box hedges. The design of one uses musical notation, the spaces filled with soft lavender and santolina. The other section is the famous Garden of Love. The designs of the four sections of this garden represent different forms of love, the passionate, the adulterous, the tragic and the tender, each with its different colored flowers. In the spring the flowers are forget-me-nots and pansies, wallflowers and tulips while in the summer, dwarf dahlias fill in the spaces outlined by the box.

This section is surrounded by trained limes and the water garden canal runs through it, part of the irrigation system of Villandry. A large lake, shaped like a classical mirror, on the upper level of the garden acts as a reservoir, the decorative equivalent of the farm duckpond.


## LOIRET

CHATEAUNEUF-SUR-LOIRE
Château, 1 Place A.-Briand, 45110 Châteauneuf-sur-Loire. Tel: 38 58 41 18.

*In the centre of the town. Parking space through the large iron gates.(70 A1)*
*Opening hours: permanently. E. Free. Wheelchairs, part is accessible. Toilets.*

Only the domed rotunda, now the town hall, some outbuildings and an orangery remain of the château that was described as a 'miniature Versailles'. The garden had been designed by Le Nôtre, but, like the château this disappeared during the Revolution. After that turbulent and unhappy time, the park was bought by a local municipal architect who remade it in the English style that was then fashionable. A stream and cascade and an avenue of limes still remain and the rest of the park was planted with 450 different species of trees and shrubs, including over 30 different oaks, magnolias and 60 different hawthorns as well as rhododendrons and azaleas. Many of these have now disappeared or, like the rhododendrons, reverted. The rhododendrons and azaleas that do remain have flourished and present a fine display at the end of May.

LES GRANDES BRUYERES
45450 Ingrannes. Tel: 38 57 12 61. Fax: 38 57 11 79.

*Ingrannes is north-east of Orléans. Leave the city on the N60 towards Châteauneuf-sur-Loire and Montargis. Then after 21 km turn left on to D921 to Fay aux Loges and Ingrannes. (69 F1)* **Opening hours:** *Two to three Sundays a month from March to November. These are fixed at the beginning of each year and tourist offices at Orléans and Châteauneuf-sur-Loire should have details.* **E.** *Moderate. Wheelchairs, possible.*

As its name Les Grandes Bruyères, (the Great Heathers), implies, the most renowned parts of this garden are the large island heather beds containing great quilts of more than 300 different heathers in pink, white, red, mauve, violet with leaves of green, gold, sage and pine. They grow magnificently well in the light sandy soil.

But there are many other plants as well. Rhododendrons, berberis, magnolias and conifers give height to the heather beds while near the house is a formal, terraced area with box-edged beds filled with hebes and teucrium. Clematis and old roses are particularly well represented and climbing roses are shown at their best on a pergola.

A 40 ha arboretum contains trees from all over the world, from areas with climates similar to that at Les Grandes Bruyères, and includes collections of cornus and magnolias.

PARC FLORAL DE LA SOURCE
45072 Orléans. Tel: 38 49 30 00. Fax: 38 49 30 19.

*Leave Orléans on the N20, south to Bourges. On reaching the outskirts of the suburb of Olivet, come off right to make a left turn towards Sully on the D14. The Parc Floral is on the left and is well signed. (69 E1)* **Opening hours:** *Every day 9-7.* **E.** *Very moderate for gardens alone; moderate for gardens and new Butterfly labyrinth. Wheelchairs. Toilets.*

Think of the RHS gardens at Wisley, then add a small train, mini-golf, deer, ducks, flamingos, a château with a formal, box *parterre* and large *miroir d'eau* and you will get some idea of what the Parc Floral de la Source is like. The 'source' is the source of the river Loiret, a mysterious bubbling spring that fills the pool in front of the château.

Around and beneath the permanent planting of avenues of cedars, poplars and taxodiums, rhododendrons and azaleas, are great changing displays of flowers. 100,000 bulbs, 70,000 biennials and 600 kinds of iris in spring, are succeeded by 90,000 bedding plants and 400 different rose cultivars. There is a *Concours* of Roses where the visitor is invited to give an opinion of the new ones on display. Later on there are dahlias, chrysanthemums and fuchsias in flower.

There is also an alpine border, rock garden, vegetable garden, many flowering shrubs and several herbaceous borders. Two small circular gardens are particularly interesting, one planted very excitingly with a mixture of grey-leaved plants and yellow flowers, the other with herbs. The iris collection is extremely good with many beautiful varieties and there is also an interesting collection of grasses. Blue and yellow conifers are planted in striking groups and pergolas are covered with climbing roses and clematis.

From July to September, the new Fleuroselect varieties are on show with the very latest in begonias, geraniums, petunias and French marigolds.

South-west of the centre of Orléans is the **Jardin des Plantes**. Greenhouses look on to a flat central area with bedding plants and then on to a broad shrub border. At the far end is the **Municipal Roseraie** containing hybrid teas, climbing and pillar roses, as well as some older roses, set out in an attractive way.


## LOIR ET CHER

PARC BOTANIQUE DE LA FOSSE
Fontaine-les-Coteaux, 41800 Montoire-sur-le-Loir. Tel: 54 85 38 63. Fax: 54 85 20 39.

*Montoire is about 45 km north west of Blois. At Montoire take the D917 to Troo, but after La Touche, take the D94 to Fontaine-les-Coteaux.(67 2F).* **Opening hours:** *Guided visits on Saturdays, Sundays and holidays, Easter to 30 September at 2.30 and 4.30; in July and August, at 3 on Wednesday, Thursday and Friday (if not a holiday) in addition; 1 to 31 October, at 3 on Saturday, Sunday and holidays.* **E.** *Expensive. Toilets (and shelter).*

The park covers 25 south-facing hectares and has been in the same family since 1751. An earlier Gérard advised the Empress Josephine on her plantings at Malmaison and, like the generations before and since, was responsible for introducing newly discovered trees and shrubs to La Fosse. At the beginning of the nineteenth century A. S. Gérard improved the buildings and added a belvedere and an orangery. During the same period, cedars, parasol pines and oaks were planted around the house.

Magnolias, cornus and rhododendrons are all spectacular in spring while lagerstroemias, ceanothus and actinidia grow against walls along with crinums, amaryllis and nerines which flourish in the protected positions and give an exotic effect in summer. *Parrotia persica, Nyssa sylvatica,* and *Carya ovata* with their underplanting of cyclamen, provide color in the autumn and in the winter the bright barks of *Acer griseum, A. hersii, Prunus serrula, P. maackii, Betula hersii, B. albosinensis* and *Arbutus andrachne* ensure that the park is as attractive then as it is in the rest of the year.


## FRANCHE COMTE
Map: see page 86


## DOUBS

JARDIN BOTANIQUE BESANCON
Place Leclerc, 25000 Besançon. Tel: 81 83 21 70.

*A very difficult town for the motorist with elaborate one-way systems. Make for the 'Parking Glacis' which is well signed (the Botanic Garden is not) and then walk up, across the busy Place du Maréchal Leclerc to the prison-like building opposite with a rockery - this is the university's department of botany. The department is situated where the Promenade de Glacis, the enormous grassed ramparts, end. (89 E1)* **Opening hours:** *Every day from 8-7; greenhouses, 8.30-11 and 2-4.30, weekdays and Saturday morning. E. Free. Wheelchairs.*

A bedding display with a difference invites the visitor into the botanic garden during the summer: pink, white and red begonias are used the illustrate the principle of plant genetics in a Mendelian Garden.

Between the building and the road are a large rock and alpine garden, with some herbaceous plants. Between the science block and the railway line are narrow order beds with medicinal and aromatic plants, ecological sections with a bed of endangered regional plants, a damp green fernery, a large bed with ornamental herbaceous and annual plants, pools with water plants and three glasshouses. There are three sections to the glasshouses - tropical, temperate and cold - plants range from coffee, banana, and vanilla to a *Victoria amazonica* water lily,succulent and carnivorous plants.

The **Promenade Micaud** and the **Promenade Chamars** are both public open spaces in Besançon. The Promenade Chamars has the distinction of being one of the first public promenades in France while the Promenade Micaud has some handsome trees, including an enormous *Sophora japonica* 'Pendula', hornbeams by the river, bedding plants and a rocky grotto

# JURA

## CHATEAU D'ARLAY
39140 Arlay. Tel: 84 85 04 22. Fax: 84 48 17 96.

*Take the Dole-Besançon road out of Lons-le-Saunier, the N83, and after 10 km turn left on the D120 to Arlay - a very interesting and attractive village. The château is on the left on entering the village. (89 D4).* **Opening hours:** *Park and château, 1 May to 15 June and 15 September to 1 November, Wednesday, Saturday, Sunday and holidays, 2-6. 15 June to 15 September, every day 2-6. E. Park and mediaeval ruins, inexpensive.*

The remains of a Gallo-Roman fortress of the Princes of Orange have been used as the central feature of a romantic landscape park that covers the hill behind the château.

A steep path zig-zags up through dark woods, leading to the remains of a chapel, with a ninth century pillar, a ruined village with its one restored cottage and the ramparts of the ancient ruined *château fort*. The fort was built on the top of solid Roman foundations - part of a wall and the cistern can still be seen. At the top there is a wonderful view over the château vineyards and the hills and forests of the Jura. On the way down the path leads by a grotto and a tiny *théâtre de verdure* or open air theatre where, in the eighteenth century, performances took place. From the grotto is a vertiginous slope that descends in grassed terraces down to the rear of the château.

In the seventeenth century, the château used to be a monastery but it was restored in 1774 by the Countess de Lauraguais who created the gardens in the then fashionable romantic style. She was luckier than many of her contemporaries and did not have to build ruins for they were already there. Even the grotto was converted from a quarry that had earlier provided stone for the château terrace.

The château is a working vineyard producing many fine wines including the unusual yellow wine peculiar to this region and has recently added a display of birds of prey in the mediaeval fortress to its attractions.

# LIMOUSIN
Map: see page 83


## HAUTE-VIENNE

### JARDIN DE L'EVECHE AND JARDIN BOTANIQUE, LIMOGES
Place de l'Evêché, 87000 Limoges .

*In the cathedral precincts. The cathedral, easily seen and well signed, is to the south east of the town by the River Vienne. (110 B2)* **Opening hours:** *Every day, 8-sunset. E. Free. Wheelchairs. Toilets near the cathedral.*

The Jardin de l'Evêché, the Bishop's Garden is the name given to the part of the garden which faces the Episcopal palace, now a museum. It was restored in 1976 to a more fitting eighteenth century style with *parterres,* pools and tree-lined walks.

Plantsmen and gardeners will find the adjoining botanic garden very rewarding. Sheltered by the massive walls of the cathedral are order beds, a collection of conifers, a water garden, shrub borders, and many climbers. The conifers, mainly smaller varieties, include *Cryptomeria japonica* 'cristata', *Cephalotaxus harringtonia* 'Fastigiata' and the handsome spreading golden yew, *Taxus baccata* 'Dovastonii Aurea'.

The order beds contain many plant cultivars as well as species. The Limoges botanic garden is a good place to compare gentians, or fuchsias or penstemons, see old friends like *Gillenia trifoliata* and make new discoveries. There are many interesting shrubs, like the rarely planted *Alangium platanifolium, Dipelta floribunda, Calycanthus floridus* and *Lonicera involucrata ledebourii* with yellow flowers and red bracted black fruits at the same time. The border of climbers contains clematis species, *Akebia quinata* and honeysuckles as well as the rarer *Holboellia coriacea* from West China. The modern water garden is attractive with seven square interlocking pools planted with aquatic and marginal plants.

Also in Limoges is **Parc Victor-Thuillat** (north of the town centre, on the Poitiers-Bellac road, shortly after the Place Sadi Carnot). This is a well-maintained municipal park in the English style: grass, tall trees well spaced and winding paths. There is a good water feature, planted with bold masses of herbaceous plants - day lilies, irises, peonies, lupins, poppies, marguerites and coreopsis - contrasting with the foliage of gunnera, bullrushes, the glaucous grass, *Helictotrichon sempervirens,* and red-leaved *Lobelia cardinalis.*

To find the **Municipal Roseraie,** leave Limoges on the N41, signed to the airport, Angoulême and Niort. Just past the sign for the end of Limoges, turn left into the Rue de Colbert. The Roseraie is signed. Like the other municipal parks it is open all the time and entry is free.

On this very open site, with its numbers of seats and scattered birch trees, right on the edge of Limoges, there is a good collection of roses, old and new. In the first beds there are old and species roses, all dated and their type given, like 'Rose de Puteau', a damask of 1768. The following beds are of more modern roses that are rare in cultivation, like 'Primavera' a pale yellow climber from 1929 and the pink pillar rose 'Tausandschon', from 1906. A pergola of climbing roses, 'Albertine' and 'Paul's Scarlet', leads on to the modern climbers and beds of hybrid teas. For anyone in or near Limoges, the municipal rose garden is worth seeking out.

PARC DE MONT-MERY
87240 Ambazac. Tel: 55 56 60 01.

*16 km to the north east of Limoges on the N20 and then the D914. At the traffic lights in Ambazac take the left turn through the village. (110 B1)* **Opening hours:** *1 March to 30 November, every Sunday and holiday, 2-6. E. Moderate..*

The 17 ha park at Mont-Méry was designed at the end of the last century by the American landscape designer, F. L. Olmstead for porcelain manufacturer, T. Haviland. In a magnificent setting it contains a collection of American plants unique in France. There are avenues of kalmias, pieris, birches, including the cherry birch, *B.lenta,* and also collections of cornus, hydrangeas, roses, including old and species roses, sequoias and cedars.

There are three linked ponds,  a sinuous river *à l'anglaise* and several *fabriques:* a bulding known as the Fairy Lodge, an eighteenth century grotto on the edge of the lake and an eleventh century motte. The château itself is in the New York Beaux Arts style and contains porcelain, books and woodcarvings collected by Théodore Haviland.

There are large plant sales at Mont-Méry in May and in October every year.

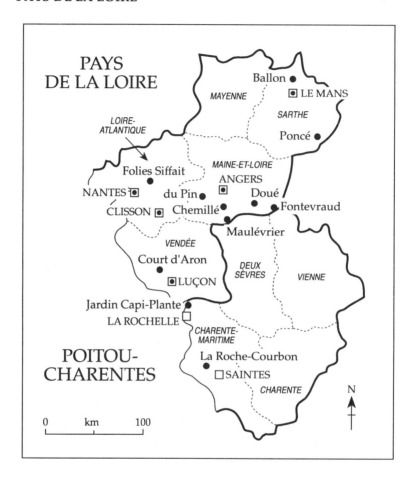

**LOIRE ATLANTIQUE**

JARDIN DES PLANTES, NANTES
Rue Gambetta, 44000 Nantes.

*Opposite the station and to the east of the Ducal château in the centre of the town.
(79 D1)* **Opening hours:** *Last Sunday in March to 31 May, 8-8; 1 June to 31
August, 8 am-9 pm; 1 September-last Sunday in month 8-8; last Sunday in
September to beginning of March, 8-6; March, 8-7. The same hours apply to all
Nantes parks. E. Free.Toilets. Wheelchairs.*

The botanic garden, with greenhouses containing cacti, palm trees, collections of bromeliads and orchids, philodendrons and peperomias, and the order beds, is but a section of the Jardin des Plantes. The order beds contain 153 species of medicinal and toxic plants and a collection of endangered species from the *Massif armoricain*.

The garden has streams, pools and cascades, the usual bedding, rhododendrons and roses and 380 different camellias. Four types of *Illicium*, the anise trees, are to be found there, along with the Californian sassafras, *Umbellularia californica*, another strongly aromatic tree.

Nantes and its Jardin des Plantes is particularly connected with the discovery, import and introduction of the magnolia to Europe. The first *Magnolia grandiflora* was brought to Nantes by a sailor from Virginia in about 1711. The Mayor of Nantes appropriated it and planted it under glass in his estate. It grew well but did not flower and after 20 years he threw it out. Happily, the wife of the gardener rescued it and planted it outside in her garden and there it flowered, amazing everyone with its enormous flowers and heady perfume. It is thought that the magnolia here in Nantes, planted in 1807 after being cultivated for 20 years, is the oldest in Europe.

For several years the Jardin des Plantes has not had the space for the new varieties of magnolia and the almost complete collection is to be found at the Parc de la Beaujoire.

PARC DE LA BEAUJOIRE
Route de St Joseph de la Porterie, 44000 Nantes.

*Take the D178 out of the town to Chateaubriant. After the Eglise St Georges and the bridge of the Boulevard A. Fleming, take the first turning on the left, the Boulevard de Beaujoire. Opening hours as the Jardin des Plantes.*

There are two sections of this park, the exhibition ground and the floral park. The floral park extends along the banks of the river Erdre and the Nantes magnolia collection of 75 varieties is based here and it is well worth seeing. There is also a good iris garden, and 730 different herbaceous plants, nearly 300 conifers and a heather garden with a very modern layout, providing inspiration for anyone planning such a garden. A recent addition is the rose garden for the Biennale Internationale de la Rose Parfumée.

Also in Nantes are:

**Parc de la Gaudiniere,** Rue de la Patouillerie, 44000 Nantes.
(Take the N137 signed to Rennes. La Gaudinière is on left just before Notre Dame de Lourdes). Originally an 18th century garden created by rich shipowners and plantsmen, it has been opened to the public since 1937. The garden is crossed by a small stream which has waterfalls here and there.

**Parc de la Chantrerie,** Rte de Gachet.44000 Nantes.(6 km north of town centre. Take the D178 to Chateaubriant, to Ecole Veterinaire.) A riverside park with a collection of about 20 bamboos.

**Parc Proce,** Place Raymond Poincaré, 44000 Nantes. (North-west of the town centre. Go towards the Cité des Dervallières, the D101 to Vannes and Redon and it is on the right, at Place Paul Dounier, with an imposing entrance.) Collections of rhododendrons, oaks, magnolias and a remarkable *Liriodendron tulipferum* opposite the eighteenth century château.

**Le Grand Blottereau,** Boulevard Auguste Péneau, 44000 Nantes. (East of the town centre. From the station continue east along Boulevard E. Dalby. Turn left to the military hospital and then left again into Boulevard A. Péneau.) A pleasant eighteenth century building with orangeries and pavilions. In front of the château is a *jardin à la française* with bedding, grass *parterres* and clipped evergreens. There are also greenhouses with a collection of tropical and useful plants.

## LES FOLIES SIFFAIT
Cellier, 44850 Ligne.

*Leave Nantes by the N23 to Angers. After nearly 25 km from the centre the road passes through the hamlets of La Barre Peinte, la Maladrie and la Vrillière. Just after the last hamlet, take the first turning to the right, towards Saint-Meen, les Génaudières. After 2 km, in the village of Saint-Meen, turn right. In 100 m is a path, GR3, which leads directly to the lower part of the Folies Siffait. (64 C4)* **Opening hours: All the time E. Free.**

A garden for the romantic, the dedicated and the energetic. The follies of M. Siffait are a succession of terraces, staircases, belvederes and archways now ruined but once forming an amazing hanging garden above the banks of the river Loire.

The garden, created at the end of the nineteenth century, is now overgrown. Under the limes and chestnuts, whose tall bare trunks give the effect of a vaulted cathedral, viburnums and laurels together with some surviving garden shrubs like lilac and cherry laurel, form an almost impenetrable undergrowth. The walls and steps that remain are thickly covered with moss and ivy. It is all mysterious and absolutely fascinating with much to discover hidden in the dim green light.

There are also plantations of horse chestnut and sweet chestnut, set out geometrically and with one or two specimen trees, like *Cedrus atlantica glauca*. The majority of the trees are lime, oak, elm, ash and hornbeam.

It would be unwise to visit this garden alone, or if you are not agile, as the scattered stones and mossy stairs can be slippery.

## GARENNE LEMOT - CLISSON
44190 Gétigné. Tel: 40 03 96 79. Fax: 40 03 99 22.

*30 km south east of Nantes on the N149 at Gétigné just beyond Clisson. Well signed. (79 E2)* **Opening hours:** *Park, every day, April to September, 9-8; October to March, 9-6. La Maison du Jardinier, April to September, every day 10-1 and 2-6; October to March, closed on Mondays. E. Free. Wheelchairs, part is accessible.*

The town of Clisson was razed to the ground during the Revolution in the wars of the Vendée and was rebuilt afterwards in an Italianate style. The sculptor Frédéric Lemot and the brothers Cacault returned from Italy after the Revolution and Lemot bought the estate of Le Garenne with its fine views over the town of Clisson. With the Cacault brothers and local architects and artists he designed temples and grottoes, columns and statues. A Temple of Love, a Temple of Vesta and *le bain de Diane* are amongst the many *fabriques* to be found in the park surrounding the arcaded villa and the Italian-rustic Maison du Jardinier where there is an exhibition about the park as well as temporary exhibitions.

## MAINE ET LOIRE

## CHATEAU D'ANGERS
49000 Angers.

*The huge thirteenth century château with its curtain wall over 1 km round and its 17 towers, is in the centre of Angers, well signed and difficult to miss. (65 F3)* **Opening hours:** *Palm Sunday to 31 May, 9-12.30 and 2.-6.30; 1 June to 15 September, 9-7; 16 September to Palm Sunday, 9.30-12 .30 and 2-6. Closed on 1 January, 1 May, 1 November, 11 November and 25 December. E. Moderate. Wheelchairs, limited access only. Toilets.*

The first part of the garden, the traditional *parterre* of clipped box and bedding plants in the dry moat round the château can be seen from the château car park. Its bold elaborations and well-chosen colors look very jolly at the foot of the enormous curtain wall.

Inside the castle, the entrance court is planted with a formal grass *parterre* boldly ornamented with arches of clipped yew, a perfect complement to the massive castle. On the ramparts, completely invisible from below, is a tiny garden, bordered with santolina, *Festuca glauca, Teucrium fruticans* and lavender and full of old roses, tradescantia, hollyhocks, achilleas - flowers represented in fifteenth century Mille Fleur tapestries. Also on the ramparts are rows of vines. There are other gardens inside the walls making the château worth a visit for these alone.

JARDIN DES PLANTES, ANGERS
Place Mendès-France/rue Boreau, 49000 Angers.

*Off the Boulevard Carnot behind the Centre de Congrès, which is well signed. The Boulevard Carnot runs into the Boulevard St Michel, the main road to Tours and Le Mans. (65 F3)* **Opening hours:** *Every day. Summer 8-8, winter 8-5. E. Free Wheelchairs.*

A very pleasant public park in the English style, with good plants. Bedding plants are subsidiary to a framework of rare trees, shrubs and herbaceous plants used for foliage effects.

Just behind the Centre de Congrès is a good planting of hostas and day lilies around ponds and waterfalls. *Cercis siliquastrum, Tilia mongolica, Celtis australis, Acer saccharinum* 'Wieri', *Ostrya carpinifolia* and *Maclura pomifera* are just a few of the unusual trees seen here. They are underplanted with rhododendrons, azaleas, peonies, camellias and *Hydrangea* 'Tricolor', giving year round interest.

JARDIN BOTANIQUE, ANGERS
16 Boulevard Daviers, 49000 Angers.

*On the opposite side of the river from the château, just as one leaves the one way system after crossing the Pont de la Haute Chaine and on the right. The Ancien Hospital St Jean which contains the Lurçat tapestry museum is opposite.(65 F3).* **Opening hours:** *Every weekday, 9-12 and 2-7. E. Free. Wheelchairs, parts are accessible.*

The botanic laboratory of the University of Angers School of Pharmacy is responsible for this botanic garden with its 3,000 species arranged in narrow beds. With order beds, of mainly medicinal plants, the Jardin Botanique complements the other two gardens in Angers.

JARDIN DES PLANTES MEDICINALES, CHEMILLE
49000 Chemillé. Tel: 41 30 35 17.

*Chemillé is south of Angers on the N160, and 22 km north of Cholet. The garden is attached to the Hotel de Ville, or town hall. (80 B1)* **Opening hours:** *All the time. E. Free.*

The small town of Chemillé is the centre of a region which has traditionally grown medicinal plants and this newly created herb garden is designed to display them. It is small, a sloping site with winding paths and irregular beds, giving a range of growing conditions for the 300 species of medicinal and aromatic herbs. The adjoining Albarel building is a documentation and tasting centre.

JARDIN DES ROSES
49700 Doué-la-Fontaine. Tel: (Syndicat d'Initiative) 41 59 11 04.

*19 km south west from Saumur along the D960 to Cholet. The rose garden is well signed in the town. (81 D1).* **Opening hours:** *Every day, permanently. E. Free. Wheelchairs. Toilets .*

Doué-la-Fontaine is the centre of a rose growing and nursery gardening area and the garden is a permanent exhibition area for local rose growers. (There is also a temporary exhibition in July in the town.)

The garden is laid out in what was once a château garden and there are two attractive pavilions  near the front entrance. The moat is planted with interesting shrubs and herbaceous plants. Most of the roses in the garden are modern, with the creations of the Meilland family well represented, and there are many climbing and pillar roses, grown on poles and pergolas, as well as cluster flowered and hybrid teas.

√ ABBAYE ROYALE DE FONTEVRAUD
49590 Fontevraud l'Abbaye. Tel: 41 51 71 41.

*Take the D751 between Saumur and Chinon and turn south mid-way, onto  the D947 for 4.5 km. (81 E1)* **Opening hours:** *Every day. 1 June to third Sunday in September, 9-7; the remainder of the year, 9.30-12.30 and 2-6 or until dusk.. Closed 1 and 11 November, 25 December and 1 January. E. Guided tours of Abbey, moderate. Wheelchairs. Toilets.*

This re-creation of a mediaeval garden round the important abbey where four of the Plantagenet kings and queens are buried - Eleanor of Aquitaine who retired there, Henry II, Richard Coeur de Lion, and Isabelle, widow of King John - was first opened to the public in 1988.

There are four separate sections of the garden: a *jardin bouquetier* to provide flowers for the altar; a *jardin médicinal et condimentaire* containing herbs for medicinal and culinary use; a *verger,* or orchard, with fruit and nut trees, and a large *potager.*

Much historical research has gone into the selection of plants used in the gardens and only plants that were available up to and including the time of the Plantagenets have been chosen.

There is a permanent exhibition about plants and gardens in the  middle ages. Plans are in hand to add another garden to this complex, this time a seventeenth century park to reflect another great period in the abbey's history when the four daughters of Louis XV were educated there. It was looted and partly destroyed during the Revolution. The abbey then became a prison in Napoleonic times and remained one until 1964.

## PARC ORIENTAL, MAULEVRIER
49360 Maulévrier. Tel: 41 55 50 14.

*Maulévrier is 13 km south-east of Cholet on D20. The old château is now part town hall and part school and the new entrance to the park is past the building and through the cultural centre next door. (80 B2)* **Opening hours:** *Every day from May to September, Tuesday to Friday, 9-12 and 2-6; Monday and Saturday 2-6; Sundays and holidays, 2-7; October to April, everyday except Monday, 2-6.* **E.** *Very moderate. Wheelchairs. Toilets.*

Parc Oriental

The Parc Oriental is the largest Japanese style park in Europe and was built between 1900 and 1913 by M. Alexandre Marcel. It is a stroll garden, a form of garden devised in seventeenth century Japan, usually around a lake with islands, where the visitor is encouraged by a series of artefacts or plants, to stroll round and discover a succession of unfolding views. Between 1880 and 1920 many Japanese gardens were created in Britain - it was the height of fashion - but few of them were entirely successful. This French-Japanese garden has been carefully restored and is particularly interesting as a representation of the Japanese garden, as a relic of European garden fashion, and for the beauty of its Khmer buildings.

There is a long walk from the new access gate to the central lake that was created by the damming of the river Moine. The Khmer bridge is the first of the oriental artefacts that is reached followed by a small pagoda that was built in 1903 and first used as an office by M. Marcel and now containing a little museum. The garden round this pagoda is a contemporary garden and contains a lantern, one of the ten scattered round the garden. A small green pond is edged with irises and other marginal plants.

The Khmer temple has four large figures at each corner and an exquisite frieze of dancers on the pediment. Inside is a statue of the Buddha. The temple was part of the Cambodian exhibit at the 1900 World Fair and is a reproduction of one of the thirteenth century temples from Angkor Wat.

The garden is not only statues, and temples. There are spring flowers and good autumn colors. At the very end of the lake there is a terraced hillock covered with azaleas and a pergola covered in blue and white wisteria.

√ CHATEAU DU PIN
49170 Champtocé-sur-Loire. Tel: 41 39 91 85

*West of Angers. Take the N23 to Nantes and Champtocé is after about 25 km. The château is outside the village.(65 E4).* **Opening hours:** *Saturday, Sunday and holidays, 2-6.* **E.** *Very moderate. Wheelchairs, part is accessible.*

The influence of Gertrude Jekyll and Edwin Lutyens can be felt in this garden created in 1920 by Gerard Grignoux. It is his grand-daughter, Jane de la Celle who looks after the garden today. One of the garden's most exciting features is the immaculate topiary that surrounds the lily pool.The garden is a series of terraces and garden rooms linked by paths or water. The formal structure is complemented by a rich planting, including mixed borders, a salvia collection, yellow roses contrasted with lavender and acanthus, delphiniums, which gives each section its own atmosphere.Beyond the formal gardens, there is a grassed area with handsome trees, then a wood from where the valley of the Romme can be seen. There are plant sales in May and November.

## SARTHE

### DONJON DE BALLON
72290 Ballon. Tel: 43 27 30 51.

*20 km to the north of Le Mans on the D300 to Mamers. (51 D3)* **Opening hours:** *15 July to 5 September from 2.30-6. E. Château, moderate. Slightly less for garden only. Wheelchairs.*

The keep or donjon of Ballon dates from the twelfth century and has the original Renaissance garden within the walls. The views are splendid. This interior garden has unusual angular *parterres* and is home to a collection of cranes and other interesting birds. The rose garden, with 125 different old and species roses, is at its best in June and July.

The building is surrounded by a 2 ha botanic park containing collections of *malus* and *prunus* that blossom in February and March together with *parrotia* and *acers* that color in the autumn. There is an unusual collection of *rubus* and striking groups of *Eremurus, Heracleum* or Giant Hogweed, *Thalictrum delavayi, Trachystemon orientalis* and *Macleaya cordata.*

### JARDIN DES PLANTES, LE MANS
4 rue de Sinault, 72000 Le Mans.

*To the east of the cathedral. If entering Le Mans from Paris, Angers and Orléans, turn right at the Etoile, before the cathedral, and turn down Rue des Arènes into the Route de Premartine. (51 D4)* **Opening hours:** *Every day 7.30-sunset. E. Free. Wheelchairs.*

A shady public park, designed in 1851 by J.C.A.Alphand who was responsible for the Parc Montsouris and the Buttes Chaumont in Paris.

At the entrance is a mediaeval solar clock in cast iron. Under the liquidambar, *Magnolia grandiflora, Sorbus torminalis* and other attractive trees there are rhododendrons, eleagnus, laurel, choisya, philadelphus, wiegelia and a collection of ferns indigenous to the Sarthe region. There is also a grotto with running water, artificial rocks and cascading streamlets.

### CHATEAU DE PONCE
72340 Poncé-sur-le-Loir. Tel: 43 44 45 39.

*Between Le Mans and Tours on the D304/D29 is La Chartre-sur-la-Loir. Take the D305 to the east to Poncé-sur-le-Loir. The château is on the far side of the village. (67 E2).* **Opening hours:** *1 April to 30 September, every day 10-12 and 2-6. Sundays and holidays 2-6.30. E. Moderate. Toilets. Wheelchairs.*

An eighteenth century labyrinth of clipped hornbeam hedges is the main feature of the garden of this sixteenth century château although the magnificent Renaissance staircase inside the château should not be missed.

At the entrance to the garden, there is a large pigeon loft to the left and then a simple grass and box *parterre*. Beyond that are the tunnels, round towers and little enclosures of the labyrinth, made entirely from hedges of hornbeam. Behind, parallel with the château, is a series of terraces with trained vines, backed by hanging beechwoods.

## VENDEE

LA COURT D'ARON
85540 Saint Cyr-en-Talmondais. Tel: 51 30 86 74.

*On the D949, 13 km from Luçon on the road to Les Sables d'Olonne. (92 C1). Opening hours: 1 April to 30 September, 10-12 and 2-6 or 7; July and August, 10-6 or 7. E. Moderate. Wheelchairs. Toilets. Restaurant.*

The extensive water gardens are the high point of the floral park that has been developed round the château of Court d'Aron. This is especially true in July when the lotus flowers are at their finest and the water lilies, iris, pontederia and other marginal and aquatic plants are adding their supporting notes. The water is alive with frogs and the flicker of damsel flies and the effect is magical.

The rest of the garden is rather curious - a mixture of the formal and informal. Winding paths through woodland planted with rhododendrons, hydrangeas and azaleas are lined with bedded-out ranks of busy lizzies, fuchsias and sweet williams. Even Iceland poppies lose their delicate charm when planted in rows.

There is a good rose garden, many dahlias on display in season and some herbaceous beds and borders, but even here, a pleasing arrangement of day lilies, alstromeria, verbascum and *Salvia sclarea turkestanica* had a prim edging of waxy begonias.

In the spring, massed bulb plantings provide the color. Like the Parc Floral at Dampierre, the Court d'Aron is the work of Dutchman Johannes Matthijsse, and the displays echo the Dutch bulbfields. This is a garden of colorful flowers *en masse*.

There is an aquarium, a restaurant and an exhibition area.

JARDIN DUMAINE
3 rue de l'Hôtel de Ville, 85400 Luçon.

*The garden is behind the town hall to the right of the D949 from Fontenay and La Rochelle to Les Sables d'Olonne, past the cathedral and the main post office. (92 C1)* **Opening hours:** *1 April to 30 September, 7.30-9pm; 1 October to 31 March, 7.30-7. E. Free. Toilets. Wheelchairs.*

A public park with a little of everything. A group of yews dating from 1830 makes an evergreen tunnel on the right of the gate while opposite it an octagonal pond with water lilies and a fountain decorated with a frog and nymph, flower beds and an attractive bandstand jostle for attention.

A hybrid *jardin anglais-français* (straight paths bounded by high box hedges, pleasant natural lake and romantic waterfall that you can walk under) leads to the *grand pelouse*, a vast lawn enlivened with little rondels of brilliant bedding plants and figures from the fables of La Fontaine created from clipped shrubs, yews and *Helichrysum petiolatum*. Vegetable giraffes, storks, donkey carts and deer stalk each other across the grass.

On the far side of the lawn there is a mount and a small greenhouse hung with bougainvillea and set about with orange trees in boxes.

## POITOU CHARENTES
Map: see page 108

### CHARENTE MARITIME

JARDIN CAPI-PLANTE
Laboratoires Capi-Plante, 21 Rue Léonce Vieljeux, 17137 Nieul-sur-Mer. Tel: 46 37 90 00.

*The manor house is in the centre of Nieul which is north of La Rochelle. (92 C3)* **Opening hours:** *Easter to All Saints. Monday to Friday, 9-5. Closed August and Public Holidays.Telephone call recommended E. Inexpensive. Wheelchairs.*

This beautiful formal garden, once known as Logis de Nieul, surrounded by groves of pines, birch, poplars and limes, was rebuilt after the war by M. Wailly and was then perfectly maintained by its subsequent owner, M. Vieljeux. It is now owned by a public company and happily they are continuing to share the garden with visitors.

Curved steps lead to a gravel terrace, edged with a low hedge of *Lonicera nitida* and decorated with pots of aloes and geraniums. The first *parterre* is very geometric, with square, box-bordered beds further emphasised by tiny parallel lines of lavender. A row of conical yews draws the eye to the statue at the end of the lawn. More long rectangles of box filled with hibiscus, are backed by hedges of hornbeam. A vista through some tall yews ends at a pedestal with an urn on it. A square pool at the end is overlooked by a statue of Neptune while, to one side, a short walk is bordered by red Japanese maples. Another vista, from a semi-circular yew hedge with a pillar at each end, looks directly to a group of dark red *Prunus cerasifera* 'Pissardii'. Along one side is a planting of conifers of contrasting shapes and colors, the bed edged with rue, agapanthus and sedum.

To the side of the house is a flower garden, with brick paths, and yew, box and lavender surrounding a circular raised pool. The beds around are filled with romneyas, irises and hollyhocks and the atmosphere is that of a country garden, in contrast to the aristocratic formality of the main section.

This is a fine example of a French post-war garden, with exquisite detailing and understated but modern, planting.

## CHATEAU DE LA ROCHE COURBON
17250 St Porchaire. Tel: 46 95 60 10.

*Take the D122 east and north at St Porchaire, which is on the N137 midway between Saintes and Rochefort. The château is well signed. (106 C1)* **Opening hours:** *Every day 9-12 and 2-6.30 (5.30 in winter).* **E.** *To park and garden, moderate. A few francs extra for the château and museum of prehistory. Wheelchairs, most is accessible. Toilets.*

The feudal château was built in the fifteenth century on a site that has been inhabited since prehistoric times. The garden, designed originally in the Le Nôtre style in 1665 when the castle was transformed from a fortress into a more elegant dwelling, is a formal layout of steps, topiary, water and terraces.

The garden of La Roche Courbon has been subject to dramatic swings of fortune. The marshy valley that surrounds the château and is the site for the formal garden is continuously trying to reclaim its own. By 1908 the gardens had all but disappeared: the woods surrounding the castle had been cut down and the river had returned to its ancient course, bringing back the marsh. Then poet Pierre Loti made a dramatic appeal for its restoration in *Le Figaro,* describing it as a 'Sleeping Beauty castle' awaiting a return to life. Eventually it was bought by the present owner's father, M. Chenereau, in 1920, and the process of restoration began.

Ferdinand Duprat, who had been a pupil of Henri Duchêne, was called in to create a new garden. He decided to make an exact replica of the 1665 garden, but to extend it over the marsh land. It was not long before one of the little watch towers, erected by Duprat at the corner of the elegant T-shaped pool which reflects the château, began to tilt. The wooden walkways that were above the water in 1935 were 1.5 m down in the silt by 1976. So, in 1978, the process of restoration had to begin all over again. Photographs illustrating the history of the garden are on show in a fascinating exhibition in the garden loggia. The firm of Delbard have donated150 trained apple and pear trees for the newly made orchard.

To learn the history of this garden is to marvel even more at the orderly but imaginative design, with its splendid steps and immaculate topiary. The shallow streams at the far end of the garden, bordered by alders and poplars and alight with butterflies and dragonflies have an added significance: the tension between nature and art here is almost palpable. The 800 m walk through the woods to the grottoes is well worth the effort. Mysterious caves are to be found at the foot of a limestone cliff in the heart of the silent woodland that surrounds the château.

## RHONE ALPES

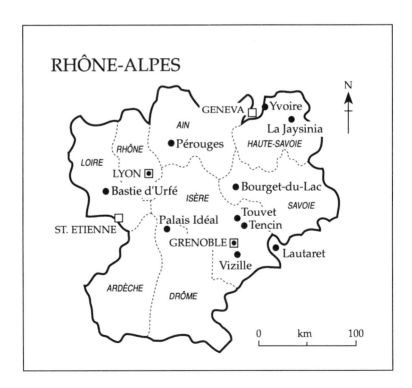

**AIN**

LES HORTICULES, PEROUGES
Maison des Princes, Rue des Princes, 01800 Pérouges.

*35 km. north east of Lyon.(116 C1) The Maison des Princes is in the centre of the mediaeval city of Pérouges. **Opening hours:** Every day from Easter to 15 October, 10-12 and 2-6. **E.** Inexpensive and includes museum, Maison des Princes and the Tour du Guet. Wheelchairs, with difficulty. Toilets, nearby.*

The three small box *parterres* which make up the hortulus have been re-created from documents and archeological traces dating from the Middle Ages. One , called the *Jardin d'Amour* contains lilies, peonies and violets between the box hedges; the other two *parterres* are of medicinal plants and culinary plants.


**DROME**

PALAIS IDEAL DU FACTEUR CHEVAL
26390 Hauterives. Tel: 75 68 81 19. Fax 75 68 88 15.

*28 km north of Romans-sur-Isère on the D538 or 11 km south of Beaurepaire. Well signed in the village. (130 B1) **Opening hours:** Every day, April to September, 9-7; October,November, February and March, 9.30-5.30; December and January, 10-4.30. **E.** Very moderate. Wheelchairs.*

This strange construction in the small garden behind the house of Hauterives' postman, the Facteur Cheval, hardly qualifies as a garden. It is a bizarre curiosity, built bit by bit over many years by M. Cheval, who brought back smooth round stones from the river in his post bag every day after he had delivered the mail The addition of 4,000 sacks of cement resulted in an edifice, reminiscent of the temples of Angkor Wat, covered with strange figures and incised with aphorisms, exhortations and symbols such as 'In creating this rock I wanted to prove the power of the will' and 'God protects genius'.

The surrealist artist André Breton was particularly attracted to its extreme eccentricity, its grottoes and tunnels, tiny bridges, balconies and circular stairs, encrusted with figures of gods and goddesses, Egyptian mummies, antlers and urns all made of bits of stone and cement. Many French gardens stretch the British conception of what a garden is, but none more so than the Palais Ideal.

## ISERE

### JARDIN DES PLANTES, GRENOBLE
Boulevard Jean Pain, 38000 Grenoble.

*Opposite the Grenoble Hôtel de Ville and Parc Paul Mistral, on the N90 to Chambéry. (131 E1)* **Opening hours:** *Every day 7.30-sunset; closing hour given on gate. Greenhouses and rock garden, 8-11.15 and 1-3.45. E. Free. Wheelchairs.*

A small public park with interesting greenhouses and a rock garden, children's games and some well labelled and unusual trees and shrubs including an imposing clerodendron, enormous specimens of *Populus lasiocarpa* with its fine large leaves, *Juglans nigra*, (black walnut), a hickory and *Picea orientalis*. Other plants of interest include a *Torreya californica*, a *Diospyros virginiana*, the heavily fruiting *Viburnum hupehense* and a *Vitex agnus-castus*. There is also a collection of fuchsias.

### PARC DU CHATEAU DE TENCIN
38570 Goncelin. Tel: 76 41 36 04.

*East of D523 midway between Chambéry and Grenoble. Both the autoroute A41 and the N90 go along the valley west of the river Isère, which can be crossed at several places, including the village of Tencin. The park is at the Grenoble end of the village, with the main gate on the left. (117 F4)* **Opening hours:** *Monday to Saturday 7-7. E. Free. Wheelchairs.*

A stately English-style park, planted with cedars set in a meadow studded with wild salvias, euphorbias and colchicums. A long, grassed terrace is lined with orange trees in pots; hanging chestnut woods form a backcloth. The retaining wall is covered with virginia creeper, brilliant red in autumn. From the terrace there is a splendid view of the Grande Chartreuse, whose majestic cliffs tower up on the other side of the valley beyond the river. Everything around the château is very simple and very bold complementing the mass of the cliff opposite.

### CHATEAU DU TOUVET
38660 Le Touvet. Tel: 76 08 42 27.

*The village of Le Touvet is just west of the N90, midway between Chambéry and Grenoble. Follow the signs to the château from the main road on the Chambéry side of the village. (117 F4)* **Opening hours:** *Guided visits, July and August, every day except Saturday, 2-6; Easter to All Saints, Sunday and holidays, 2-6. E. Gardens only, inexpensive.Wheelchairs, parts are accessible.*

The Château du Touvet is in a splendid situation on the west side of the valley of the Isère, gazing over towards the Alps. An avenue of chestnuts

122

leads towards the forecourt and the bridge that crosses the L-shaped pool, where the waters that flow from sheer sides of the Grande Chartreuse are temporarily captured before they flow further down the valley. On the right a circular building guards the *cour d'honneur*.

From here there is a good view of the famous cascade, the water staircase where the mountain spring water bubbles and skips its way down over ledges and into a series of ornamental ponds.

There are also classical *parterres*, box-edged beds filled in summer with standard roses and begonias - unfortunate in a classical garden with surroundings of such unspoiled grandeur. Nearer to the château is a tiny garden, surrounded by a wall pleasantly covered with vines and *Clematis montana* and with a strip of hostas at the foot.

## DOMAINE AND CHATEAU DE VIZILLE
38220 Vizille. Tel: 76 68 07 35.

*16 km south of Grenoble - the Route Napoleon, the D5 via Eybens is pretty. The château is in the centre of the town. (131 E2)* **Opening hours:** *Every day except Tuesday and 1 May. April to May and September to October, 9-7. June to August 9-8; November to February 10-5. E. Free. Wheelchairs. Toilets. (Not recommended)*

The huge château that contains the Museum of the Revolution has a fine staircase coming down from the building to ground level. The park is planted with groups of trees and has a long canal down the centre, a *miroir d'eau* and bold groups of fountains. It also offers pony trap rides, a fish farm and a zoo. Surrounded by steep, tree-covered hills, the park is a pleasant place to walk in but not notable as a garden.


## LOIRE

### LA BASTIE D'URFE
42130 Saint-Etienne-le-Molard. Tel: 77 97 54 68.

*50 km north-west of St Etienne on the N82 and then west at Feurs on the N89. Turn left at La Maison Blanche to St Etienne-le-Molard. (115 D2)* **Opening hours:** *Every day, except Tuesday, 9-11.30 and 2.30-5.30. E. To château and garden, moderate. Wheelchairs. Toilets.*

The château has a magnificent arcaded double loggia around the *cour d'honneur*. Inside the château but open to the air, is one of the earliest grottoes in France, built in imitation of those in Italy. It has delicate ironwork grilles of vines and trellis and is entirely covered with shells, in compositions which evoke pagan mythological figures.

Outside there is a simple box-edged *parterre* with conical yews and a central rotunda with semi-circular arches supported on Ionic columns. The statue of Autumn gives the temple its alternative name of the Temple d'Automne but it is also known as the Temple of Love.

## RHONE

### PARC DE LA TETE D'OR
Boulevard des Belges/Boulevard Stalingrad, 69459 Lyon.

*1.5 km north of the town centre, on the banks of the Rhône, opposite the Palais de la Foire. Route Bourg-en-Bresse, the N83, is the way to go from the city centre. Vehicles can enter the Boulevard de Stalingrad under the railway lines. Metro station: Massena. (116 A2)* **Opening hours:** *1 April to 30 September 6am-10pm; 1 October to 30 March, 6am-8pm. The botanic garden, 8-11.30 and 1-5. Greenhouses, every day from 9-11.30 and 1.30-5. The Alpine Garden, 1 March to 31 October, 8.30-11.30. The Rose Garden is open at the same times as the park. E. Free. Toilets. Wheelchairs. Refreshments.*

The Parc de la Tête d'Or is the only large public park in Lyons and, as such, it is a social and recreational centre as well as a horticultural one. In addition to the botanic garden, rose garden and greenhouses, there are picnic areas, a guignol or puppet theatre, a huge lake with pedaloes, mini-pedaloes and fishing; pony rides, little cars and trains, animals, miniature golf, go-karting and kiosks selling food and drink. The park was designed by the Bühler brothers at the time of the Second Empire. It is typical of its time, with a vast circular walk round the perimeter, lawns dotted with clumps of trees and many cross paths and *allées*. The main entrance has large, exuberant iron gates made at the beginning of this century.

The greenhouses, originally built in the nineteenth century, were reconstructed in 1972 and are reputed to have one of the richest plant collections in Europe. Tropical and sub-tropical plants including orchids and succulents, and the famous *Victoria amazonica* giant water lily can be found here.

There are three separate sections of roses: a collection of 570 species and varieties in the botanic garden; a rosarium in which the annual competition for the finest rose in France takes place and a new International Rose Garden. This last is a modern, naturalistically landscaped area and includes a long pergola to support climbing and rambling roses and modern reconstructions of classical pergolas.

The botanic garden contains about 15,000 species of plants arranged according to habitat or geographical region. The alpine garden has about 2,000 plants. There is also an arboretum and a large lake.

It was an early gardener in the park, M.J. Chretien, who first coined the term *mosaiculture*, a mixture of carpet bedding and flower bedding. There are many examples in the park.

## SAVOIE

### LE BOURGET DU LAC
Place de l'Eglise, 73370 Bourget-du-Lac.

*Le Bourget-du-Lac is 10 km north of Chambéry and the garden is behind the church. (117 E2) **Opening hours:** All the time. E. Free. Toilets, inside the château-priory only. Wheelchairs.*

The centre piece of this terraced formal garden is the topiary garden, where yew trees have been clipped to resemble pieces on a chess board. A central *bassin* and fountain add sparkle and movement while rare tree species surround the formally composed grass and box-edged areas. The eleventh century priory and its fifteenth century cloister, together with the garden, are a sharp contrast both to the hub-bub of today and the wildness of the surrounding mountains.

## HAUTE SAVOIE

### LA JAYSINIA
74340 Samoëns. Tel: 50 34 49 86.

*In the centre of Samoëns, to the right of the pharmacy at the west of the church. (105 E3). **Opening hours:** All year 8-12 and 1.30-7. (1 October to 30 April, 5.30) Saturday, 8-12. E. Free. Wheelchairs - there is access and the main path has a good surface, but it is very steep. Toilets.*

This precipitous alpine garden was the brainchild of Marie-Louise Cognacq-Jay, a native of Samoëns and, with her husband, founder of the Samaritaine department store in Paris. It was laid out in 1905-6 by Louis-Jules Allemand and opened in September 1906. In spite of being abandoned during and after the first world war, the garden never became irretrievably derelict. In 1988, a great deal of work was done in the garden and the adjoining laboratory in honour of the 150th anniversary of Mme Cognacq-Jay's birth.

A wide, well-surfaced path zig-zags up the mountain, by the side of a rushing waterfall. Stony paths lead off this main path between the different beds where plants are grown in sections, representing eight geographical areas and four distinct habitats. Indigenous trees, pines and birches, and small shrubs, (e.g. *Salix retusa, Ribes alpinum*, the pink flowered *Sorbus chamaemespilus, Coronilla minima* and *Abies pinsapo* from south west Europe), cling to the steep rocky slopes while alpine plants from all regions of the world are tucked into every crevice and pocket of soil.

There are many seats in the garden where the views of Samoëns and the surrounding alps together with the background noises of cowbells and rushing water can be appreciated. Near the laboratory building are slopes of the tiniest alpines, androsaces, silene, saxifrages, cushions of minuartia, minutely flowered *Helianthemum canum* as well as some beautiful *Meconopsis napaulensis* and many different hieraciums, all underplanted with spring bulbs.

Any alpine gardener will find this garden very well worth visiting, but, like the English alpinists who first discovered the many attractions of the region in the 1850's, they will also find that a degree of fitness is necessary to enjoy it fully.

LE LABYRINTHE - JARDIN DES CINQ SENS
74140 Yvoire. Tel: 50 72 88 80. Fax: 50 72 90 80.

*On the shores of Lake Geneva (Lac Léman). The prettiest way is to take the D25 along the shore towards Thonon-les-Bains, via Anières and Hermance on the Swiss side of the border or east from Thonon on the N5 to Geneva and then a right turn on to D25 at Bonnatrait. The old part of Yvoire is pedestrianised so park at the first car park and enter through the first gateway. (104 B2)* **Opening hours:** *Every day, mid-April to mid-May, 11-6; 16 May to 18 September, 10-7; 19 September to mid-October, 1-5. E. Moderate. Toilets. Wheelchairs.*

Opened only at the beginning of May 1988, this pretty garden in the *potager* of the château is a delightful oasis in the middle of a village smothered in scarlet geraniums. This garden of the five senses was designed by Alain Richert. The garden is small but there are many interesting features and ideas for the gardener. It is a delightful place just to sit and gaze at the colors, enjoy the scent of the plants and listen to the bird song.

The first feature to be seen is a rectangular bed planted with vivid green festuca grass; a large rock off-centre, contributes to the Japanese effect. In the spring the grass is studded with gentians, saxifrages and fritillaries and the area is like an alpine meadow. The next plot is mediaeval in style, a criss-cross pattern of rustic and sophisticated plants - glaucus avena grass and the white rugosa rose, 'Blanc double de Coubert'. A tiny herb garden - four beds around a fountain - forms a place for meditation similar to those found in the gardens of the middle ages.

The main part of the garden is the labyrinth of hornbeams with a central aviary whose inhabitants add the sound to this garden of the five senses. It has four sections: a garden of textures, one of colors, one of taste and one of scents. The garden of textures contains plants with interesting leaves: artemisias, inulas and hellebores, while the garden of taste has fruit bushes, strawberries, rhubarb, celery and much else. Daphnes, lilies, roses, honeysuckle and violets are the backbone of the perfumed garden and the color garden is full of geraniums, gentians, iris and campanulas.

Round the old walls are ancient fruit trees, a persimmon and a large old lagerstroemia. A collection of clematis has been added to these, and at the foot of a shady wall, ferns and hostas grow. The lovely *Gaura lindheimeri* seeds itself in the paths. An old cherry tree supports a 'Kiftsgate' rose.


**HAUTES ALPES** (Provence-Côte d'Azur)

JARDIN ALPIN DU LAUTARET
05220 Col du Lautaret par le Monetier-les-Bains.

*On the N91, 90 km from Grenoble and 30 km from Briançon. Strictly speaking this garden should be classed under Côte d'Azur-Hautes Alpes, but it is covered here as it is so far from the other gardens of the Riviera.* **Opening hours:** *Last Sunday in June to first Sunday in September, every day 10-6.30. E. Moderate. Wheelchairs. Toilets in nearby café.*

There are more than 2,000 species of alpine meadow and rock plants in this garden in the mountains where the Dèpartements of Isère, Hautes Alpes and Haute Savoie meet. The garden is the property of the medical and scientific University of Grenoble and is laid out in a naturalistic way around the laboratory.

There are plants from all the mountainous regions in the world - the Carpathians, the Rockies, the Pyrenees, the Himalaya and the Atlas together with the mountains of the southern hemisphere. Pines like *Pinus mugo uncinata* and *P. cembra*, willows, including *Salix lapponum, S. serpyllifolia* and *S. herbacea*, larch, juniper and rhododendron give a more permanent framework and some shelter to the smaller plants in the very harsh climate, where the temperature can be as low as 4°C in July.

Among the plants from North America are *Epilobium luteum, Dicentra formosa oregona, Caltha palustris palustris* with large leaves and flowers 7.5 cm across and the rose-colored *Sedum rhodanthum*. From the alps come the campanulas *C. alpestris, C. cenisia,* and *C. thyrsoides*, the brilliant blue *Eritrichium nanum* as well as peonies, poppies, iris and *Aquilegia alpina*. A rarity from the alps to look out for is *Saussurea depressa*.

No lover of alpine plants should miss this garden in its magnificent setting a few kilometres away from the foot of a spectacular glacier.

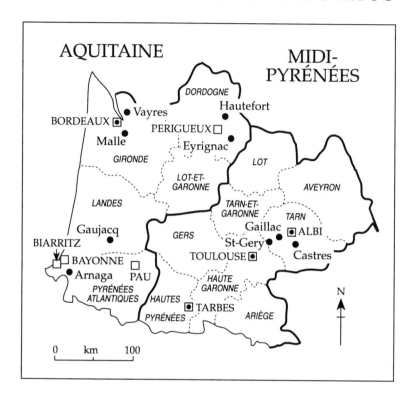

## AQUITAINE

### DORDOGNE

CHATEAU DE HAUTEFORT
24390 Hautefort. Tel: 53 50 51 23.

*76 km south of Limoges. Leave Limoges on the N20 to Brive-la-Gaillarde and after 2.5 km take right fork the D704 to St Yrieix-la-Perche and Hautefort. The château is visible from a great distance and is well signed. (124 A1)* **Opening hours:** *Palm Sunday to All Saints 9-12 and 2-7. All Saints to Palm Sunday, Sunday 2-6.* **E.** *To park and garden, moderate. Toilets. (Inside château). Wheelchairs.*

The splendid mass of the Château de Hautefort dominates the rich wooded countryside of the Dordogne for miles around. At the entrance, very simple but bold *parterres* of green and variegated box, filled with catmint and hypericum and a long covered walk of clipped thuya complete with windows and a rotunda at the end, perfectly match the château in scale and drama.

On the other three sides of the château, the box *parterres* are more elaborate. Each bay seems to have its own pattern, formal, geometric yet very varied and all immaculately maintained. When there are bedding plants their use is dramatic and straightforward with the bronze-foliaged scarlet dahlia, 'Bishop of Llandaff' or canna lilies in blocks of bright color. Elsewhere large clipped yews in a variety of comfortable shapes - cottage loaves, drums, domes, mushrooms - complement low, formal *broderies* of box.

Across the bridge, away from the formal garden, some shrub planting quickly gives way to a wooded park. Here clearings are carpeted with columbines, purple orchids, violets and wild strawberries and a broad mossy path winds down to the valley and the village below.

Château de Hautefort

## JARDINS DU MANOIR D'EYRIGNAC
24590 Salignac-Eyvigues. Tel: 53 28 99 71. Fax: 53 30 39 89.

*Near Salignac-Eyvigues between Sarlat and Brive-la-Gaillarde on D60. Well signed. (124 B3)* **Opening hours:** *Every day; 1 April to 31 May, 10-12.30 and 2-7; 1 June to 30 September, 10-7; 1 October to 31 March, 10-12.30 and 2-dusk.* **E.** *Moderate. Wheelchairs possible. Toilets.*

The manor of Eyrignac is a charming country house in the Perigord style, dating from the seventeenth century.

The gardens are on three levels, rising from the back of the house and are in the classical French tradition, composed of box, yew and hornbeam but with statues, vistas and tall cypress trees that give an Italian effect. Like many gardens *à la française,* they were turned into an English style park and planted with trees in the nineteenth century. The present enchanting garden is a re-creation that reflects the spirit of the original.

There is one long vista from the house where two parallel flights of lichen-covered stone steps lead to a lawn embroidered with delicate lines of box and surrounded by flower borders in tones of white, yellow and blue. The lawn is followed by a long, stepped walk, bordered by clipped yew obelisks. There are two fine axes to the left of this walk. One cross axis is the *Allée des Vases,* punctuated with Italian pots; another cordonned by elegantly clipped hornbeam leads past a swimming pool with its eighteenth century pavilion to a Chinese pagoda. From the *Pavillon de Repos,* there is a fine view over the countryside. With the largely evergreen planting, this beautifully structured garden is a pleasure to visit at any time of the year.


## GIRONDE

### JARDIN BOTANIQUE, BORDEAUX
Terrasse du Jardin Public, Place Bardineau, 33000 Bordeaux.

*Behind the orangery in the Jardin Public, off the Cours de Verdun. Drive along the Quai de la Douane, past the Bourse; turn left at the Grand Théâtre and at Place de Tourny take the main road to Le Verdon. Turn right into rue de A. Barraud and then into Rue de la Course, where it is possible to park (121 D3)* **Opening hours:** *Every day, 8-6.* **E.** *Free. Wheelchairs. Toilets.(expensive)*

There is an attractive iris border in the Jardin Public itself but it is the botanic garden behind the elegant orangery which is of particularly absorbing interest. At the centre is the water garden with a collection of water lilies, *Nymphoides peltata* and lotus and marginal plants. The order beds contain cultivars as well as species and are especially interesting for gardeners. Families are presented systematically (Engler's classification) and the beds

Jardin Botanique Bordeaux

contain such diverse plants as a fine *Pterocarya stenoptera* and *Asimina triloba. Magnolia denudata, M. acuminata* and *M.* x *soulangeana* and species dahlias like the magnificent *D. imperialis, D. coccinea* and *D. scapigera*. Many species of clematis are represented. Rarer plants are an *Idesia polycarpa* and *Eucommia ulmoides*, the only hardy tree to produce rubber. Many plants are acclimatised here, but local flora is equally important. Also in Bordeaux is the spacious well treed **Parc Bordelaise**

CHATEAU DE MALLE
33210 Preignac. Tel: 56 63 28 67.

*Leave Langon, 47 km south-east of Bordeaux, by the D116 to Arrancon and Landiras and as soon as the motorway has been crossed, take the first turning on the right and go back under it to Malle. (135 E1)* **Opening hours:** *Easter to 15 October, every day except Wednesday, 3-7. 1 July to 31 August, 10-7.* **E.** *Moderate. Toilets.*

Set in the middle of the vineyards of Sauternes and Barsac, the Château de Malle has the distinction of having an Italian garden unlike any other in France. The château was built in the seventeenth century but, in 1702, one of the heiresses of Pierre de Malle married an Italian and so Italian ideas and

131

craftsmanship were absorbed into the design of the garden and its statues. A handsome wrought iron gate leads to the U-shaped château with a central three-storey section and single storey wings with pepperpot towers. Small groups of stone figures decorate the gateposts and are echoed by those statues that stand at regular intervals round the garden.

At the back four terraces rise up away from the house. A long, grassed terrace ends in a balustrade decorated with urns and cherub, from which one can look over the vineyards below. At the other end of this terrace is a small colonnaded grotto, the Italian theatre, decorated with shells and pebbles and containing statues of figures from the *Commedia dell' Arte*, the popular comic theatre of Italy, and mythology. The top terrace has ten figures that stand sentinel over the garden, statues that represent local activities, many connected with the vine and winemaking but also hunting, fishing, the harvest and music making.

A visit to this unusual and charming Italianate garden can be combined with a purchase of some of the château's excellent wine.

CHATEAU DE VAYRES
33870 Vayres. Tel: 57 74 85 15.

*Leave Libourne on the N89 to Bordeaux and after 6 km turn right on to the D242 to Vayres. (121 E3)* **Opening hours:** *Sundays and holidays all year 3-4 and 5 in summer. 1 July to 31 August, every afternoon, guided visits to château and gardens at 3, 4 and 5.* **E.** *Moderate. Toilets.*

The garden in front of the crenellated château is Italian in inspiration with an elaborate staircase leading to the *parterre*. A double flight of steps curves round a small grotto, descends to a single flight then follows a small bridge over the empty moat to another double flight and a smaller single flight. The staircase seems to be all in one with the central storied dome of the château. A formal grass *parterre* with clipped yews in a variety of conical and rotund shapes leads from the château down to the River Dordogne. At the side of the garden there are two long double hedges of hornbeam complete with buttresses and arches, giving an architectural effect.


## LANDES

CHATEAU ET PLANTARIUM DE GAUJACQ
40330 Gaujacq. Tel: 58 89 01 01 and 58 89 24 22.

*The château of Gaujacq is some way from the village, on the D58 between Bastennes and Brassempouy, south west of Mont-de-Marsan. Take the D933 between Mont-de-Marsan and Orthez; 10 km before Orthez, take the D101/D15 to Amou, then D158 towards Bastennes and Donzacq. (149 E2)* **Opening hours:** *Château* *(guided visits) 1 July to 31 August every day except Wednesday, 2.30-6.30; 15 February to 30 June and 1 September to 15 November, Saturday and Sunday 2.30-6.30. Closed from 15 November to 15 February. Botanic nursery and Plantarium: all year, every day except Wednesday, 2.30-6.30. E. Nursery, free. Plantarium and château, moderate. Wheelchairs.*

The château was built in the seventeenth century in the style of a Roman villa - a single storey arcaded building, round an interior courtyard planted with magnolias, pieris, roses and tree peonies. Lagerstroemias in red, pink and violet flower in August. On the outside is a large and very old Chinese persimmon, *Diospyros kaki*.

M. and Mme Jean Thoby run the attached nursery and are creating a botanic garden (plantarium) at the side of the château below some massive Gallo-roman ramparts. The new garden, which was started in 1986, has a formal French structure and English-style planting.

Many different types of clematis and trachelospermum are trained on the rampart walls, with Mediterranean plants at their feet. There is a panoramic view of the Pyrenees from the garden. In the arboretum area there is the national collection of pieris, an extensive collection of cryptomerias, camellias, hostas, hydrangeas and some fine acers including *Acer palmatum* 'Shishigashira' and *A.p.* 'Beni-schichihenge'.


## PYRENEES ATLANTIQUE

ARNAGA
Musée Edmond Rostand, 64250 Cambo-les-Bains.

*1 km outside Cambo-les-Bains on the D932 to Bayonne. (148 B4) Opening hours: Every day, from 1 March to 31 October, 9.30-12 and 2.30-6.30. E. Moderate. Wheelchairs. Toilets.*

Arnaga was designed by French writer Edmond Rostand. The house and garden sit rather oddly together. The house is an enlarged version of a Basque farmhouse placed awkwardly in the middle of a vast *parterre* full of formal effects that don't quite come off.

The main vista leads from the overgrown Swiss chalet to a curved pergola with a pavilion topped by a pineapple at each end. The *parterre* is bounded by a hedge and a tunnel of clipped hornbeams. The clipped trees in the *parterre* itself are too small for the very wide, flat site. The municipal planting is not good. The garden at the back of the house has some large, old trees underplanted with blue hydrangeas, rhododendrons and azaleas.

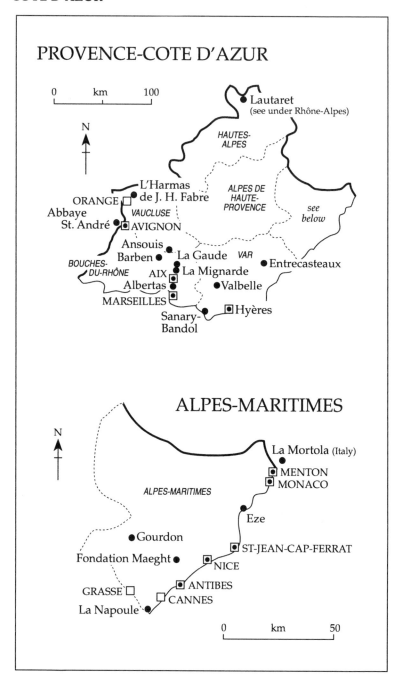

PROVENCE-COTE D'AZUR

## ALPES MARITIMES

### VILLA THURET
62 Boulevard du Cap, 06602 Antibes. Tel: 93 61 55 60.

*Take the Boulevard du Cap, which goes from south of the town along the middle of the Cap d'Antibes. The tiny path Chemin G. Raymond is on the west side and goes right round the garden which is signed on the Boulevard but cannot be entered from the main road. (165 D4) Opening hours: 8-5.30 on working days only. Wheelchairs. Toilets (In the Institute of Agronomy). E. Free*

Botanist Gustave Thuret retired to the Cap d'Antibes in 1856 and was responsible for planting the first eucalyptus there. In 1875, after his death, his heirs gave the garden to the state and it is now part of the Institut National de la Recherche Agronomique.

Thuret's garden is now past its best and has been in course of restoration since 1988. Borders have been recently planted with Australian members of the Myrtaceae (myrtles, eucalyptus, leptospermum and many others), Proteaceae (embothriums, grevilleas) and erythrina, conifers, mimosas and deciduous broad-leaved trees. However, there are still many mature specimens of palms, eucalyptus and mimosas to be seen, as well as flowering shrubs and some herbaceous plants. Particularly noteworthy are the massive elephant grey trunks of *Jubaea chilensis*, the wickerwork bark of the sabal palms and the startling whiteness of the trunks of *Eucalyptus benthami* and *E. viminalis*.

There is a collection of callistemons and a spring visit will coincide with the flowering of large free-standing shrubs of fremontedendron and *Rhaphiolepis* x *delacourii*. *Vitis voinieriana* with huge serrated leaves grows there too. This is very much a working arboretum and not a manicured garden. New plants are tested here to see if they can adapt to the region. Some of the areas are being cleared and replanted with new species that may be more resistant to disease or pests as chemicals are not used. This laudable practice means that sections of the garden look less than picturesque. However, for the botanist and plantsman there is much of interest.

### VILLA EPHRUSSI DE ROTHSCHILD
Ave Ephrussi-de-Rothschild, 06230 St Jean-Cap-Ferrat. Tel: 93 01 33 09.

*Take the turning to St Jean-Cap-Ferrat off the N98 Villefranche to Beaulieu road. At the road/railway bridge junction, Pont St Jean, take the D25 to the south, along the Cap. The Musée Ephrussi de Rothschild is well signed. (165 E3). Opening hours: Every day from 15 February to 1 November, 10-6 (7 in July and August); from 1 November to 15 February, every day from 2-6; 10-6 in school holidays and at weekends. E. Moderate. Toilets. Wheelchairs, most of garden is accessible.*

The pink and white villa stands high on Cap Ferrat, unmistakeably visible from both Villefranche and St Jean. The villa and the lovely gardens that surround it were constructed between 1905 and 1912 by the Baronness Ephrussi de Rothschild to house some of the many art objects she had amassed. The villa is now owned by the Musée de Beaux Arts. Madame Ephrussi did not only buy art objects but anything that caught her fancy: whole chapels, *bas reliefs*, pillars and statues, gargoyles and fountains. Many of these are beautifully displayed in the several gardens of different styles and periods that surround the villa.

In the entrance court to the museum there is a well from Verona, home to brilliant green, noisy, frogs and *bas reliefs* from fifteenth century Catalonia. The first of the separate gardens is the Spanish one which recalls the gardens of Aranjuez, cool with its fountains, pool and grotto surrounded by arums and papyrus. Facing across the bay to Villefranche is the Florentine garden, a composition of horseshoe shaped steps and a grotto with philodendrons and narcissi.

One of the most unusual gardens is the lapidary garden where, among the Judas trees, stand mediaeval *bas reliefs* and strange figures that were once gargoyles on church roofs.

Villa Ile de France

Then follows a Japanese garden with stone lanterns, bamboo irrigation pipes and a planting of rich green. Next comes the exotic garden, with cactus and agaves, followed by a colonnaded temple sheltering a statue. Beyond and behind this last garden is the ancient rose garden, now an English garden, with meandering shady paths and semi-wild planting. From here there are views of the other side of the headland to Beaulieu.

Immediately behind the house is the large *parterre a la française*, formal in layout but given a completely new aspect with its profusion of grey plants, santolina hedges and *Teucrium fruticans* clipped into spheres, soft against the pink and white iced cake of the villa itself. Tall palm trees instead of clipped yew complete the exotic, if idiosyncratic, effect.

This is one of the most attractive gardens in the area and well worth a visit.

JARDIN EXOTIQUE, EZE
06360 Eze

*Right at the top of the old village of Eze between Nice and Monte Carlo, in the castle ramparts and well signed. (165 E3) Opening hours: Every day,1 November to 31 May, 9-12, 2-5; 1 June to 30 September 9-8; October 9-5 . E. Inexpensive.*

A wide range of cacti and succulents well displayed among the ruined ramparts of the ancient château. The views are spectacular and worth the climb.

FONDATION MAEGHT
06570 Saint-Paul-de-Vence. Tel: 93 32 81 63.

*Just outside the village of St Paul on D7. Well signed. (165 D3) Opening hours: 1 October to 30 June from 10-12.30 and 2.30-6; 1 July to 30 September, 10-7. E. Expensive but includes galleries. Toilets.*

The terraced sculpture garden set around the Maeght Foundation's Gallery of Modern Art, contains sculptures by Giacometti, Miro, Barbara Hepworth and Alexander Calder among others. The pieces are well displayed, above shallow pools with floors of tiles or slate slabs where the water ripples and reflects the light and the sculpture, or in courtyards between the various wings of the building, or on lawns beneath large pine trees.

A garden for the designer and art lover, with good views of the surrounding countryside.

## CHATEAU DE GOURDON
06620 Gourdon. Tel:93 92 50 13.

*14 km north east of Grasse . Take the D2085 and then turn left after Magagnosc, following the D3 towards Gréolières. (164 C3)* **Opening hours:** *1 June to 30 September, 11-1 and 2-7, every day. From 1 October to 31 May, every day 2-6 except Tuesday.* **E.** *Inexpensive*

The terraced gardens were designed by Le Nôtre and are on three levels above a high precipice yet all within the walls of the château. A small white garden can be seen through the gates of the château, beyond the terrace. There is a box *parterre* in the *cour d'honneur*, a mediaeval apothecaries garden and an Italian garden. A path of crazy paving, unusual in France, curves alongside the interesting half-moon shapes of the *parterre* with its mop-headed lime trees. The Italian garden can only be seen from above. However, there is a splendid view and an exhilarating contrast between the formal clipped evergreens and the landscape of Provence .

## LES COLOMBIERES
Route des Colombières, Boulevard de Garavan, 06500 Menton. Tel: 93 41 62 48.

*Through Menton towards the Italian border. At the Port of Menton Garavan, at the beginning of the new port, turn left into the Route du Pian. Turn right at Boulevard de Garavan and then first left. The road is narrow, steep and has some sharp bends. (165 F3)* **Opening hours:** *1 January to 30 September every day, 9-12 and 3-sunset* **E.** *Moderate. Toilets. Refreshments.*

The slightly ramshackle appearance of Les Colombières as it is today, does not detract in the least from its unique charm. Indeed, for anyone with romantic inclinations, the crumbling *fabriques*, the gnarled and leaning trees, the enthusiastic undergrowth actually increase the beauty of the garden. It is a garden that is poised on that narrow edge between picturesque neglect and the slide into dereliction, however, and should be visited without delay.

Les Colombières is the only remaining complete garden designed by the painter and garden designer, Ferdinand Bac. Bac believed in using the indigenous flora of the coast and the natural provençal stone but he was also a great traveller and was much influenced by his journeys around the Mediterranean. Thus brilliant ceramics appear in unexpected places in the steep, hillside garden, giving a Moorish effect. He also uses a particular deep terracotta for some of the balustrades, temples and viewpoints, which he believed went specially well with the deep green of the cypress trees. The result is a fascinating garden, rambling up and down the hillside and with many unexpected corners, several inspired by the works of classical philosophers: Homer's garden, the Philosopher's Stair and Orpheus' rock.

Every few yards there are panoramic views of old Menton and the Italian riviera.

Amongst the cypress trees is supposedly the oldest carob, *Ceratonia siliqua*, in France. The garden is redolent with the scents of pine, lavender, cypress and rosemary and occasional groups of shrubby echiums compete with the vivid colors of the ceramics.

In season, a small tea room overlooking a pool and surrounded by murals of the life of Ulysses is open. It is also possible to see some of the magnificent ground floor rooms in the house, designed and painted by Ferdinand Bac himself. Not to be missed.

LE JARDIN BOTANIQUE, VAL RAHMEH
Avenue St Jacques, 06000 Menton. Tel: 93 35 86 72.

*In the district of Garavan to the east of Menton. Follow the Promenade du Soleil to the Porte de France and turn left after the Church of St Jacques, into Avenue St Jacques. The road is a cul-de-sac and the Jardin Botanique is at the end. There is no parking in grounds, but there is a turning circle in road outside.(165 F3)* **Opening hours:** *Every day , 1 May to 30 September, 10-12 .30 and 3-6; 1 October to 30 April, 10-12.30 and 2-5. E. Inexpensive. Toilets. Wheelchairs part is accessible.*

The Jardin Botanique Exotique is a paradise for the plantsman and flower-lover. Although there had been a garden at Val Rahmeh since the beginning of the century. and indeed, the villa had been once leased by Lord Radcliffe, it was not until it was bought by Miss 'Maybud' Campbell in the mid 1950's, that it really became a botanic garden. Miss Campbell, a botanist who had worked at the British Museum (Natural History), added hundreds of species to the garden. In 1966 it passed to the French National Museum of Natural History and an enthusiastic staff keep the garden well-maintained and constantly renewed.

An avenue of palm trees leads to the villa from the road and outside the building are a brick paved terrace and a small *parterre*, home to clumps of strelitzias. The walls of the villa are covered with exotic climbers, *Distictis buccinatoria* with blood red flowers, yellow at the base, *Beaumontia grandiflora* with white trumpets, and the bright scarlet flowered *Dicliptera suberecta*, all interspersed with climbing geraniums. Behind the house, tall clipped cypress hedges are festooned with *Tropaeolum pentaphyllum* and form a background for a row of terracotta pots.

Brugmansias (daturas) in variety, including *B.sanguinea, B.chlorantha*, and *B. 'Grand Marnier'*, all the size of trees, grow near the balustrade at the end of the *parterre*. The balustrade which overlooks the pool and water garden with lotus flowers and water lilies, is covered with white *Rosa laevigata* while climbing up the same wall from below is a bougainvillea with a trunk nearly three feet wide.

There are palms and aloes, including several chorisia species with spiny trunks, and the umbrella-like *Oreopanax echinops*. At their best in spring are the large bushes of *Eupatorium ianthinum* with their large soft leaves and purple flowers, *Buddleja madagascariensis, Polygala myrtifolia* and *Greyia sutherlandii* with scarlet flowers in terminal racemes. Later in the year, *Lycianthes (solanum) rantonnetii* with violet-blue flowers, *Cestrum nocturnum,* the greenish-yellow flowered night-blooming Jessamine, the strongly scented *Osmanthus fragrans* and the blue flowered climber, *Thunbergia grandiflora* can be seen.

The effect of all the richly-colored, exotic flowers from all over the world is positively intoxicating almost any time of the year. April is a good time to see the flowers, but the weather can be overcast and damp.

Also in Menton are the **Pepinière Delrue,** a cactus nursery in the rue Aristide Briand and the gardens of **Fontana Rosa** created by novelist Vincente Blasco Ibanez, author of 'The Four Horsemen of the Apocalypse', and dedicated to his 'masters', Cervantes, Dostoevsky, Balzac and Dickens. This villa and garden, embellished with brilliant ceramics, has recently been restored.

LA NAPOULE
06210 La Napoule-Plage.

*On the N98, 8 km west of Cannes. (163 F3) Opening hours: Guided visits 1 March to 2 November, 3-4 every day except Tuesday. Includes château and workshops. E. Moderate. Toilets. Wheelchairs.*

American sculptor, Henry Clews Jr, bought this château, which overlooks the harbour at La Napoule-plage, in 1918. He restored the château and his wife Mary created the garden as a setting for his remarkable sculptures. It is now run as a Franco-American cultural centre.

Mary Clews devised a simple evergreen setting with great masses of dark yew and cypress, cedar and bay, underplanted with contrasting glossy-leaved ivies, box, pittosporum and euonymus, around a series of spaces containing a sarcophagus (engraved by Henry Clews with a poem to Mary), a statue or a Venetian well head. English garden designer John Brookes has added, in the Italian garden, a cool scheme of marguerites, agapanthus, santolina and *Teucrium fruticans.* With the four oleanders at the corners of the rectangular pool, it is a planting with restraint and elegance. The simplicity of the garden, with its axial design and views

La Napoule

through or over the walls to the harbour, forms a dignified setting for the disturbing intricacies of Clews's sculptures.

PARC CIMIEZ
Place du Monastère, 06000 Nice.

*Cimiez is a suburb of Nice, to the north of the city centre. Follow signs to Cimiez, Nice East and/or the Gallo-Roman remains. (165 E3)* **Opening hours:** *Every day. 1 April to 31 May and 1 to 30 September, 8-7; 1 June to 31 August, 8-8; 1 October to 31 March 8-6.* **E.** *Free. Wheelchairs, parts are accessible. Toilets .*

This publicly owned rose garden next to the Franciscan monastery and museum at Cimiez is a tranquil oasis set high above of Nice.

The stonework of the old steps and walls lifts this garden, which is basically roses and bedding, out of the ordinary. Roses are trained over arches and bowers in the French manner while a long pergola, covered with a flourishing

HAUTES ALPES

JARDIN ALPIN DU LAUTARET

This alpine garden is so near to the borders of Savoie and Isère that it is covered at the end of the Rhône Alpes section.

# ITALY

GIARDINO BOTANICO HANBURY, LA MORTOLA
La Mortola, Ventimiglia, Italy. Tel and Fax: 0184/229507.

*East of Menton. Take the left fork, the top road, into Italy and the Giardino Hanbury is on the right.after a few kilometres (165 F3) Opening hours: 27 March to mid-June, 10-6 (last visits 5); mid-June to 25 September, 9-7 (last visits 6); winter, 10-5 (last visits 4). Closed on Wednesdays until mid-June. E. Expensive. Pay in francs or in lira although change may be a problem with francs. Toilets.*

This garden, made by an Englishman in Italy is so close to the border and so worth visiting, that it seemed impossible to leave it out of this guide.

Like many of the coastal gardens along the Riviera, La Mortola is on a steep site and it is terraced from 300 feet above sea level, down to the shore. It was created by Sir Thomas Hanbury, who gave Wisley to the RHS in 1867. Sir Thomas died in 1907 - he and his wife are buried in an Indian style mausoleum in the garden - and his son Sir Cecil, another keen gardener, took it over. However, as a result of Cecil Hanbury's death just before the war in 1937, the garden eventually became the property of the Italian government who allowed it to fall into neglect. Since 1987 it has been the responsibility of the University of Genoa and things have improved.

It is still a plant-lovers' paradise with many of the exotic plants collected by Sir Thomas Hanbury from all over the world, continuing to flourish in the superlative climate. Flowering hedges of *Teucrium fruticans* and richly scented *Pittosporum tobira* are used to divide different areas. Wintersweet, *Chimonanthus praecox*, is laden with fruit and there are tree-sized varieties of spurge, acanthus and heliotrope while shrimp plants, *Justicia brandegeeana*, make great clumps in the borders.

Located on the terraces with their fountains, steps, belvederes and pools are an Australian garden with eucalyptus and callistemons, an exotic garden with agaves and opuntias, a peony garden dotted with bits of classical masonry, a flowering meadow and a grove of citrus trees. Many pittosporums prosper in the garden, like *Pittosporum floribunda* with its fragrant mimosa-like flowers and *P. crassifolium* which has small dark red trumpets. The double yellow jasmine, *Jasminum mesnyi*, grows everywhere. A simple wooden pergola is festooned with *Caesalpina sepiaria*, a climbing shrub with red-stamened yellow flowers.

At La Mortola it is possible to get quite drunk with the luxuriance of the exotic plants and some of the combinations, like the deep blue *Scilla peruviana* growing under a heavily laden tree of an extra-large grapefruit variety, the shaddock. A garden not to be missed, not only because of the wonderful plants that grow there, but because the more visitors there are, the more chance there is of the garden continuing to flourish.


## PROVENCE
Map: see page 134


### BOUCHES DU RHONE

DOMAINE D'ALBERTAS
13320 Bouc-Bel-Air. Tel: 42 22 29 77.

*Between Aix-en-Provence and Marseille on the N8 autoroute. Take the Bouc-Bel-Air exit. The garden is signed from there. (159 E3)* **Opening hours:** *June, July and August, every day 3-7; May, September and October, weekends and holidays, 2-6.* **E.** *Very moderate. Wheelchairs, most is accessible. Toilets.*

The magnificent gates of the two sections of the garden at Albertas face each other across the road from Marseille to Aix. The lower garden or Jardin du Pavillon has a central axis to the north. The upper garden relates to a château that was never built but itself remains, a remarkably intact combination of Italian garden and *jardin français*. Box hedges, Judas trees and grass are a relaxed setting for fine fountains, *bassins* and monumental statues of Hercules, Samson, tritons and gladiators. The highest terraces were probably never completed and are now shaded by trees and shrubs; places to dream in and from which to view the garden.

There is a sale of rare and mediterranean plants, an exhibition and a conference at Albertas during the first weekend in June.

CHATEAU DE LA BARBEN
13330 Pélisanne. Tel: 90 55 19 12.

*The village of la Barben is 8 km east of Salon-de-Provence on D572 through Pélissanne. The château is about 3 km beyond the village. (159 D3)* **Opening hours:** *Château, every day 10-12 and 2-5. Closed on Tuesday.* **E.** *To château, moderate. Wheelchairs, access difficult. Toilets in château.*

The Le Nôtre *parterre* with its central pool and the 200 year old sequoia and *Pinus cembra*, can be seen at their best from the wall of the ramp leading up to the château itself, before the entrance kiosk. It is not possible to go into the garden but there is a different view along the main axis from the bottom road that is signed to the adjoining view. A typically lovely Provençal setting but the garden is probably of interest only to historians.

PARC BORELY AND JARDIN BOTANIQUE E.M. HECKEL
Avenue du Parc Borely, 13008 Marseille Tel: 91 55 14 68.

*South of the city near the Plage du Prado. Coming into Marseille from Cassis turn off the D559 at the Rond Point du Prado, down the Avenue du Prado and left to the Château Borely.(160 A3) Opening hours: Park all year. Jardin Botanique, every day 10-12 and 1-6. (Sunday, pm only.) E. Greenhouses and Botanic Garden, inexpensive. Wheelchairs. Toilets. Café.. Botanic shop and exhibitions.*

Behind the Château Borely is an eighteenth century formal garden, a pool with fountains, sunken lawns with rectangular pools and a central round pond at a lower level. A circular metalled road goes round the park and curving paths and clumps of trees, designed in the landscape style by Barillet-Deschamps, make it a pleasant place in which to walk. There is a lake with boats, swans and an open air cafe beside it. Other features are a rose garden with over 900 varieties and a large cascade-cum-grotto: a romantic creation like a mossy, ferny cliff face, dripping with water.

The botanic garden has a collection of irises, 300 species and varieties, more than 300 species and cultivars of fuchsia, a garden of climbing plants that is unique in France and a garden of medicinal and aromatic plants. The greenhouse which is a cast iron structure dating from 1870 was rescued from another building and re-erected here in 1982. It contains orchids and bromeliads as well as tropical plants with edible fruits.

CHATEAU DE LA GAUDE
Route des Pinchinats, 13100 Aix-en-Provence. Tel: 42 23 11 44.

*Leave Aix on the D96 to Pertuis and Manosque. Take the right hand turn to D63C, signed to the Complexe Sportif Domaine de Tournon and Les Pinchinats 2.5. After Les Pinchinats, take the turn to Venelles. La Gaude (and La Mignarde) are on the left of this road. (159 E3) Opening hours: 1 April to 30 September, 10-12 and 3-6. E. moderate. Wheelchairs, part is accessible. Wine can be purchased.*

La Gaude is a Provençal *bastide* or country house and the garden is an exquisite example of a French formal garden on a domestic scale, part of it unaltered since its creation in the eighteenth century and guaranteed to transform any doubtful Briton into an enthusiastic formalist.

A long entrance drive of clipped box and spindle, shaded by chestnut trees, leads to a terrace closed by a wrought iron gate. A simple raised garden on the right, in front of the chapel and orangeries, is decorated with urns and troughs, prettiest when filled with delicate pale blue pansies, which, like the gentle sound of the fountains there, seem to cool the summer air. This is a recent addition.

On the left, in front of the house, is a series of terraces of differing size overlooking the countryside where the small hills give way to the abrupt slopes of Mont Ste Victoire on the horizon. On the second terrace is a 200 year old circular box *parterre*, almost maze-like in its complexity, surrounded by canals so that it is virtually an island. Bosky *parterres* at either side contrast with the clipped formality of the central labyrinth. Two narrow terraces, their walls lined with stone vases on pedestals, lead to a large lawn with geometrically arranged paths, a circular pool, and a viewpoint over the valley beyond.

The vista of the entrance *allée* is continued past the house through pine trees. On the left steps lead down to a narrow walk, the *Tèse*, bordered by shrubs, while further along on the right, there is a circular green room or *salle verte*, cut out among the trees.

The perfect proportions of the design of this garden are admirably echoed by the taste and devotion of the owners who cherish it so beautifully today.

LA MIGNARDE
Route des Pinchinats, 13100 Aix-en-Provence. Tel: 42 96 41 86.

*Leave Aix-en-Provence on the D96 to Pertuis and Manosque. Take right hand turn on to D63C signed to Complexe Sportif, Domaine de Tournon and Les Pinchinats 2.5. Drive through Les Pinchinats and take the turn signed Venelles. La Mignarde is on the left (just before La Gaude). (159 E3)* **Opening hours:** *Every day all day.* E. Moderate. Wheelchairs.

La Mignarde is a garden of statues. The original Ledoux garden with its formal layout was replaced by a *jardin anglais* but there are now only vestiges of either - avenues of trees and some terracing - but the statues remain. They are spaced round a large lawn with two pools and are attributed to B. F. Chardigny who worked in Aix around 1784. The statues are nearly all female - goddesses, nymphs and maidens in seductive poses, delicate and attractive.

On the terrace by the house is a rectangular pool and at the end of the terrace is a grotto with urns and very fine statues of Venus on a dolphin and Hercules wrestling with a lion. More friendly lions spout water as part of the fountains on the terrace. This very open garden has good views over the surrounding countryside.

147

## PAVILLON VENDOME
32 Rue Célony, 13000 Aix-en-Provence.

*West of Cathédrale St Sauveur, along the main inner boulevard. At the Etablissement Thermal keep straight as if leaving the town. The Pavillon is on the left. (159 E3)* **Opening hours:** *Every day, 9-12 and 1.30-5 . E. Free. Toilets. Wheelchairs.*

The impressive house with its imposing caryatids was built as a provincial residence for Cardinal de Vendôme, and later inhabited by the painter Van Loo. It is now owned by the town of Aix and the garden is very much a municipal facility in which people sit and toddlers play.

There is a simple grass *parterre* with clipped box and a circular *bassin* and fountain in the centre. The surrounding walls are covered with white and yellow Banksian roses in spring.


## VAR

### ENTRECASTEAUX
83570 Entrecasteaux.

*26 km west of Draguignan. Take the D562 to Lorgues and then the D50. From Aix, leave the A8 autoroute or the N7 at Brignoles. Take the D562 through Carcè s and turn left on to the D31 to Entrecasteaux. (161 D1).* **Opening hours:** *Garden open at all times; château, every day. E. Free. Wheelchairs: can not enter the garden but it can be seen perfectly from the square.*

The whole of this *parterre*, designed by Le Nôtre, can be seen from the wall in the village square. The château, beautifully restored, sits high on its rock overlooking the village and the garden, and is owned by Mr and Mrs McGarvie Munn. They once owned the garden as well but very generously gave it to the town as a public park and it is now freely open to everybody.

The simple *parterre* with its box-edged beds around a central pool and mossy fountain is shaded by some fine trees, *Magnolia grandiflora, Celtis australis* and a *Cercis siliquastrum* (Judas tree).

### CASTEL STE CLAIRE
Boulevard Edith Wharton, 83400 Hyères. Tel: 94 65 12 07.

*Take the N98 Avenue de Toulon, towards Toulon, following the signs to the château. At Rue Victor Basch, the Castel Ste Claire is signed. It is at the end of the road. (161 D4).* **Opening hours:** *Every day, 8-6. (5 in winter, 7 in high summer) E. Free. Wheelchairs possible, but it is very steep.*

American novelist and garden writer, Edith Wharton, bought Castel Ste Claire in 1919. The terraced gardens and buildings are now the headquarters of the Hyères parks and gardens department. They are very well maintained but there is nothing to remind the visitor of Edith Wharton or recall her writing on gardens. The luxuriant borders are full of large clumps of well-placed flowers, chosen for their color and scent. There are strategically placed seats, some shaded by a remarkable *Cedrus deodara*, from where one can gaze out on Hyères spread out below. Verbenas, euryops and echiums in good large groups and a *Dracaena draco* (Dragon tree) are also to be found in this well-planted Mediterranean garden on many levels.

PARC OLBIUS RIQUIER
Boulevard Ambrose Thomas, 83400 Hyères. Tel: 94 65 12 07.

*South of town towards Hyères Plage. At Place 11 Novembre, where Avenue Gambetta crosses the freeway Olbia, take the left hand fork over the freeway into the Avenue Olbius Riquier. (161 D4)* **Opening hours:** *Every day, 7.30-6; 5 in November and December; until 8 from June to August; Greenhouses, 8-11.30 and 3-6.30, closed Saturday morning. E. Free. Toilets. Wheelchairs.*

The Parc Olbius Riquier is both Hyères' botanic garden and a well-used public park, with a small collection of animals, a children's play area and a duck pond. By the entrance, a group of three weeping white mulberries, a *Yucca filifera*, the tall palm *Washingtonia filifera* and a *Cupressus torulosa* (Bhutan cypress) add an exotic note to what looks at first like an ordinary public park. In fact, everything seems to grow well in Hyères public parks and the rock garden is a good example. It is not a home for tiny alpines but is bright with arctotis, osteospermums, day lilies, *Convulvulus cneorum* and *Othonna cheirifolia* . Tender plants that need cosseting in the UK, are seen here flowering in the spring in lavish clumps.

The greenhouse has a good collection of tropical and equatorial plants and climbers. Parrots and other birds plus the constant sound of trickling water, give a real sense of being in a tropical environment. Huge strelitzias, ferns and rampaging climbers and creepers add to the effect. Look for the elegant, goblet-shaped *Chamaedorea metallica, Archontophoenix cunninghamiana*, (Illawarra Palm from New South Wales) and *Ficus lyrata*, as well as the more common hibiscus and *Solandra maxima*.

In the park there is a pond and small waterfall, bordered by a collection of irises, a *Firmiana simplex* with fine foliage, a fastigiate pedunculate oak, and a *Sapindus utilis* (probably *Sapindus saponaria* or soapberry).

## PARC ST BERNARD
Montée de Noailles, 83400 Hyères. Tel: 94 65 12 07.

*North of the old town of Hyères. Go through the Place République, turn right at the Church of St Louis, then bear left down Avenue Paul Long and left again, after some distance, along the Montée de Noailles. (161 D4)* **Opening hours:** *Every day, 8-6; 5 in November and December, 5.30 January to March and October. 7.30 June to August. E. Free*

A terraced garden high up behind Hyères, with panoramic views over the town.

The house at Parc St Bernard was built in 1925 for Charles de Noailles by R. Mallet-Stevens and its famous cubist garden was designed by Gabriel Guevrekian with the help of Jacques Lipchitz whose statue, Joie de Vivre, was used as a focal point. The garden was in the shape of an isosceles triangle that lead directly off the windows of the salon and was laid out with rectangles of flowers and colored, molten glass.

The house became a ruin, the cubist garden closed and the rest of the terraces, although containing some good trees and other plants were neglected, at least by the high standards of the rest of the gardens owned by the town of Hyères. There is good news for a generous benefactor has been found, and a use for the house (as a museum of design) so restoration is in hand.

In the lower terraced garden there is a huge magnolia as well as the rare *Xanthoceras sorbifolium*, a deciduous tree with racemes of white flowers with a carmine spot at the base, *Macfadyena capreolata*, a climber with yellow-red trumpets, and *Loropetalum chinense*, an evergreen witch hazel with white flowers. *Lonicera fragrantissima* and *Viburnum carlesii* perfume the terraces in early spring. Many other plants that need protection in Britain, brugmansias (daturas), solanums, salvias, euryops, *Cyphomandra crassicaulis* and *Exochorda korolkowii*, grow vigorously in this garden.

## JARDIN EXOTIQUE, SANARY-BANDOL
Pont d'Aran. 83110 Sanary. Tel: 94 29 40 38. Fax: 94 29 08 59.

*To the north of the A50 autoroute north of Bandol (exit Bandol). It is signed to the right off the D559 on entering Bandol from Sanary-sur-Mer. (160 C4)* **Opening hours:** *Every day, 8-12 and 2-6.(7 in summer). Closed on Sunday morning from October to the end of March. E. Moderate. Wheelchairs. Toilets. Refreshment kiosk in summer.*

This pleasant and surprisingly intimate garden is widely advertised as Jardin Exotique and Zoo. It is designed for families and can be over-run with small children so it is worth timing a visit carefully.

The cacti in the greenhouse are varied and well labelled and the orange trees, hibiscus and bougainvillea make them very attractive. Attached to the glasshouses is a plant sales area full of small versions of the tempting sub-tropical plants that are on display. There is a large rock garden and a shady botanic park.

The dark colored rosettes of the crassula *Aeonium arboreum* 'Schwarzkopf', pots of *Streptosolen jamesonii* and hibiscus all add to the exotic effect. There is also a water garden and a large rock garden.

VALBELLE
83170 Tourves. Tel: (Mairie) 94 78 70 03.

*Tourves is about 40 km east of Aix-en-Provence along the N7 to Fréjus. Take the turning to Tourves Centre and take the first right signed to Parking. Continue on foot from car park. Turn left by the trough and fountains and the path, unmarked and steep, is on the right. The obelisk is directly above. It is dangerous to go too near the ruined façades and the commune will take no responsibility for accidents. (160 C2)* **Opening hours:** *All the time.* **E.** *Free.*

The remains of the façade of this severely classical eighteenth century château tower above the little town of Tourves.

The story of Valbelle is a sad one. The young Comte Joseph-Alphonse-Omer de Valbelle, who built the château on the ruins of a mediaeval fort and created the park between 1767 and 1777, was a patron and practitioner of the arts. He was also a free-thinker and upset the villagers and the church by bringing young women of doubtful repute from Paris to act as models for figures on his own memorial. The count died young and without an heir and the building was left empty for some years. It was pulled down by the still enraged villagers during the Revolution. The château stood for everything the villagers feared and disliked about the aristocracy and having demolished it, they turned their backs on it. That dislike was still evident as recently as 1988, symbolised in the lack of notices and directions.

Only a few of the buildings from this grand eighteenth century park remain, hidden in the undergrowth and only the romantic or the historian will want to battle through the thorny scrub to search them out. The first plateau is the site of the colonnade, the obelisk and the ruins of the château. Hidden a long way behind is a pyramid and on a side road is a dairy in the form of a temple. Part of the fountain still exists, too, but has been transferred to a well in the centre of the village.

The site is a good place to look for wild flowers. Spurges, including the dark-eyed *Euphorbia characias*, grape hyacinths, valerians, orchids and rock roses as well as aromatic thymes and rosemary grow undisturbed.

## VAUCLUSE

### CHATEAU D'ANSOUIS
84240 Ansouis. Tel: 90 79 20 99.

*In the centre of the tiny hill village of Ansouis, 8 km north of Pertuis. Go north of Aix en Provence on the D556 and then take the D56 north west of Pertuis. (159 E2)* **Opening hours:** *2 January to 31 December 2.30-6. Closed on Tuesdays. E. Moderate.*

Only two sections of the much photographed hanging gardens are open to the general public on guided tours: the entrance terrace which can be seen before embarking on a tour and the *terrasse du paradis* with its high sculpted box hedges with elegant balls at each corner of the geometric layout.

### ROCHERS DES DOMS
84000 Avignon.

*In the centre of Avignon, next to the Palais des Papes. (158 B1)* **Opening hours:** *Every day 7.30-7. E. Free. Wheelchairs. Toilets. Refreshments.*

A public park with panoramic views over the Rhône, the famous bridge and Villeneuve-lès-Avignon. Stone grottoes, a large pond with ducks, a kiosk selling drinks and shady trees make this a pleasant retreat on a hot day.

### L'HARMAS DE J.H.FABRE
84830 Sérignan-du-Comtat. Tel: 90 70 00 44.

*Go north east from Orange on the D976. Fabre's house is on the right just before the village of Sérignan-du-Comtat. (144 B3)* **Opening hours:** *Every day except Tuesday and Sunday, 9-11.30 and 2-6. E. Very inexpensive. Wheelchairs. Toilets.*

Harmas comes from a Provence word that means 'an uncultivated plot' and, although this garden is full of unusual and well-labelled plants, as befits a botanic garden, the overall effect is one of semi-wilderness as its creator would have wished. Winding paths and burgeoning plants and a pleasantly casual standard of maintenance make it a fascinating garden to wander round and different plants can be discovered at every visit and in every season.

It was the garden of the great naturalist and polymath J.H. Fabre who lived until he was 92 and wrote 112 books. Most of his books were translated into many other languages and he was a friend of John Stuart Mill and Charles Darwin. The house and garden are now owned by the entomological department of the French natural history museum.

*Scilla peruviana* grows wild among the arbutus trees while *Pistacia terebinthus*, *Eriobotrya japonica,* (the evergreen Japanese loquat) and *Maclura pomifera,* (Osage orange) flourish among amelanchiers, cistus, *Euphorbia splendens* and the indigenous *Anagyris foetida* with yellow pea flowers.

Inside the house a small proportion of Fabre's exquisite water colors of the fungi of the Vaucluse can be seen, as well as copies of all his books, including many of the translations.

## LANGUEDOC ROUSSILLON

## AUDE

ABBAYE DE FONTFROIDE
11100 Narbonne. Tel: 68 45 11 08.

*14 km south west of Narbonne. Leave Narbonne on the N113 to Carcassone; after 5 km take the D613 to Lagrasse. Then, after 7 km take a small turning to the left to the Abbaye. (173 D2).* **Opening hours:** *Guided tours; every 45 minutes, 1 April to 9 July and 1 September to 31 October, 10-12 and 2-5; every half hour, 10 July to 31, 9-30-6.30; every hour, 1 November to 31 March, 10-12, 2-4.* **E.** *Moderate.*

This Cistercian abbey is situated at the mouth of one of the gorges of the Corbières. The abbey itself is one of the finest examples of Cistercian architecture in the south. The cloister with Gothic walks has an ancient wisteria; there is a replica of the garden of St Francis of Assisi, with olive trees and cypresses. To these have been added in recent years a large rose garden with over two thousand rose bushes from Delbard in beds edged with box and santolina and a small scented garden with a collection of old roses and plants of the *garrigue*.

## GARD

### ABBAYE ST ANDRE
Fort St André, 30400 Villeneuve-lès-Avignon. Tel: 90 25 55 95.

*Across the river to the west from Avignon is Villeneuve-lès-Avignon and, towering over Villeneuve is the Fort of St André. Inside the fort on the right-hand side is an inconspicuous door leading to the gardens of the Abbaye of St André. Cross from Avignon by the bridge Edouard Daladier and take the D 980 towards Orange. (158 B1)* **Opening hours:** *Every day except Monday, 10-12.30 and 2.30-6 (2-5 in winter). E. Very moderate. Wheelchairs. (parts are accessible). Toilets..*

One of the most delightful gardens in France is hidden behind the forbidding walls of the Fort of St André. The ruins and ramparts of the Abbaye were transformed into a garden at the beginning of this century by Mlle Elsa Koeberle. In the spring, perhaps the best time of year for visiting the garden, the many levels, hidden corners and unexpected walks are alight with coronilla, *Cercis siliquastrum* (Judas trees) and irises. In early summer, old roses and the main *parterre* by the entrance with pools, beds of santolina and soft pink roses, are the focuses of attention. Later flowerings are of oleander and sedums.

Intriguing pieces of wall, old statuary, even ancient sarcophagi, mingle with indigenous mediterranean plants, olive trees, cypresses and the coronilla and valerian that seed themselves everywhere.

### BAMBOUSERAIE DE PRAFRANCE
30140 Générargues par Anduze. Tel: 66 61 70 47. Fax: 66 61 64 15.

*Anduze is 13 km south-west of Alès. Take the N110 south and then turn right at St Christol-lès-Alès on to the D910. The Bambouseraie is north of Anduze at Générargues. An alternative attractive route from Alès is by the D50 Route St Jean du Pin to Générargues. (142 D4)* **Opening hours:** *Every day, March, 9.30-6,1 April to 21 September, 9.30-7. Closed Monday and Tuesday in November and December. Contact the garden for hours from 22 September. Closed January and February. Guided visits. E. Moderate. Wheelchairs. Toilets. Nursery. Refreshments.*

The Bambouseraie is unique in Europe, a bamboo forest on a large scale. It was started by Eugene Mazel in the middle of the last century. Laying on the water supplies to give the bamboos the right conditions took all his money and he died a ruined man. Luckily, after some years, another keen gardener and botanist took over the collections and it is the grand-daughter and grandson-in-law of this benefactor who continue to run the estate.

Even if you start by knowing or even caring little about bamboos, it is impossible not to become interested in them after visiting this garden. There is a surprising variety and, with their colored stems - glaucous green, emerald, yellow and black - and the special sound of the wind in the leaves, the groves are totally different from other woodlands. Strange, alien new shoots, some black with furry tufts, seem to appear from the ground and grow as you watch.

The uses of bamboo are also demonstrated here - there is a complete Asian village and the flower beds in the other parts of the garden are edged with curved bamboo canes.

Other oriental features include a water garden with water lilies and giant koi carp, a Japanese water garden and in the spring, peonies bloom. There are greenhouses filled with colorful plants and a bamboo nursery with plants for sale. Other attractions are camellias and azaleas, palm trees and the largest *Magnolia grandiflora* in Europe

JARDINS DE LA FONTAINE
30033 Nîmes.

*At the end of Avenue Jean Jaurès. (157 E1)* **Opening hours:** *Every day 1 April to 14 June, 8am-9pm; 15 June to 15 September, 7am-11pm; 16 September to 31 October, 8am-9pm; 1 November to 31 March, 8-7.* **E.** *Free. Wheelchairs, access to lower part only. Toilets nearby.*

At first all there appear to be in the Jardins de la Fontaine are stone balustrades. Look over them and you discover a series of sunken colonnades and a subterranean river. Most of the features of this central *parterre* are below ground level although there is a central fountain decorated with statues of nymphs. The water rises in a pool, the source of Nemausus, behind the nymphaeum, and the sparklingly clear water flows through the colonnades and around the garden.

The gardens were started by engineer J.P. Mareschal in the middle of the eighteenth century, when the ruins of the Temple of Diana nearby, were first discovered. They were incorporated into the plan and can still be clambered over, although the gardens were never finished.

Where further terraces should have been built, broad paths zig-zag up a steep hill clothed in evergreens, Italian cypresses, *Pinus halepensis,* and *Abies pinsapo* to the Tour Magne at the top. The paths are edged with aromatic shrubs. Trees in the gardens include *Maclura pomifera* (Osage orange), *Firmiana simplex,* with long panicles of yellowy green flowers in August, and *Albizzia julibrissin.*

In high season the garden is illuminated until 11pm.

CHATEAU DE TEILLAN
30470 Aimargues. Tel: 66 88 02 38.

*24 km north-east of Montpellier and 18 km south-west of Nîmes. Leave either the N113 or the A9 at Gaillargues for the N313 to Aigues-Mortes. 3.5 km south of town of Aimargues there is a narrow turning west to Teillan. (157 D2)* **Opening hours:** *15 June to 15 September, every day except Mondays, 2-6.* **E.** *Moderate. Wheelchairs. Toilets.*

The garden at Teillan is densely shrubby, with winding paths. Set among the viburnums, laurels and yew is a collection of Roman steles or gravestones. The first statue to be cast in cement, dated 1830, a figure of Ceres, stands by a small pool.

There are two other interesting features. First, a noria or underground well with steps down to it where the water is raised by a cast-iron mechanism of suspended buckets. The noria at Teillan is very large and was used as a Jewish ritual bath in the middle ages. The second feature to note is the *pigeonnier* or dovecote. The ground floor was once used as the local prison while the top is completely lined with pigeon nest boxes.


**HERAULT**

JARDIN DES POETES
Allées Paul Riquet, 34500 Béziers

*At the southern end of the tree-lined promenade in the centre of Béziers and with one entrance opposite the Gare du Midi.* **Opening hours:** *Every day, 8-sunset.* **E.** *Free. Wheelchairs. Toilets.*

An interesting public park designed by one or both of the Bühler brothers, with a large pond, and good trees, including zelkovas, liquidambars and *Celtis australis.* The Plateau des Poètes is the highest part of the site, a lawn where busts of regional poets are displayed on plinths. There is a striking fountain with a memorable statue of a Titan by Antonin Injalbert. Well worth seeking out if you are in Béziers.

CHATEAU DE CASTRIES
34160 Castries. Tel: 67 70 68 66.

*12 km north-east of Montpellier. Take the N113 to Nîmes and then turn left on to the N110 at Vendargues. (156 C2)* **Opening hours:** *Every day except Mondays (unless they are holidays), 2.30-5.30; guided tours at 2.45, 4 and 5.15. E. Including interior of château, moderate. Wheelchairs. Toilets.*

Originally built at the end of the fifteenth century, the château of Castries was burned in 1652 by the Duke of Rohan during the Wars of Religion. Between 1656 and 1675 the château was renovated and gardens were designed by André le Nôtre. At the same time, engineer Paul Riquet built an aqueduct 6,822 m long to bring running water to the pools and grotto. This aqueduct with its gentle gradient, is still functioning and can be seen by visitors.

One of the demolished wings of the château was never replaced and is now the site of a terrace from where one can see the two gardens. One is a simple *parterre* with two symmetrical pools and fountains and the other, at right angles to it, is an elaborate design of box *en broderie* with colored gravels in the original manner. This is reached by two ramps that lead down to the lower level and are themselves a strong part of the design, framing a dripping grotto containing a terracotta cherub. On a lower level still is a grass area with a large central *bassin* surrounded by radiating avenues of trees, designed to give a false perspective

CHATEAU DE FLAUGERGUES
1744 Avenue Albert Einstein, 34000 Montpellier. Tel: 67 65 79 64. Fax: 67 65 21 85.

*3 km east of the centre of Montpellier. Take the road to Mauguio. Cross le Pont Juvenal, and at the roundabout take Avenue Albert Einstein. After just over a mile you will find the château on your right near the Parc Club du Millenaire. It is well signed. (156 C3).* **Opening hours:** *Gardens, every day except Sunday, 9.30-12 and 2.30-7. July and August, also open Sunday pm.Tours of the château 1 July to 30 August every afternoon except Monday. Le Caveau (the wine vault) selling the estate A.O.C. wine and a shop selling local products is open every day from Monday to Saturday. E. Guided tour, moderate.*

The original *parterres* of this garden were destroyed to make a *jardin anglais* in the nineteenth century but the present owner is gradually restoring the garden to its former plan.

In front of the château is a formal *parterre*, a mixture of straight and curved lines with an astronomic ball as a centrepiece and a small *miroir d'eau*. Provençal pots in a local design, each one signed by its maker, contain citrus trees while the *parterre* is bordered by irises, peonies and oleanders. There is a cross axis where high box hedges have windows cut in them and seats are placed so that there is a view of the vines that are so important to the economy of this estate.

To one side is a park with palm trees and a small orangery. The owner is extending the planting here, adding to the bamboo, the old arbutus trees and the cedars. Other trees of interest in the garden include a large *Mespilus germanica* (medlar) , a *Maclura pomifera* and an *Acca (Feijoa) sellowiana.*

CHATEAU DE LA MOGERE
Route de Vauguières, 34000 Montpellier. Tel: 67 65 72 01.

*4 km from Montpellier. Cross the river Lez, south of the town centre, by the Pont Juvenal and continue on the Route de Vaugières, D172E. La Mogère is reached shortly after the road crosses the A9 autoroute. (156 C3)* **Opening hours:** *Pentecost to 31 September, every afternoon 2.30-6; 1 October to Pentecost, Saturdays, Sundays and holidays, 2.30-6. E. Moderate. Wheelchairs.*

La Mogère was a formal garden, constructed on symmetrical lines, with a circular *miroir d'eau* reflecting the eighteenth century château and box edged grass *parterres* leading to the terrace with its statues of shepherdesses.

The main feature of the garden, however, is the restored *buffet d'eau*. A *buffet d'eau* is a feature of garden architecture, usually placed against a wall or in a niche, over which water flows into a series of bowls or troughs. The one here is especially noteworthy. The walls and niche are decorated with orange calcite and shells, topped by statues and urns and contains the head of a mischievous looking river god.

In the overgrown park that lies to the right of the château there is a miniature aqueduct that was built at the beginning of the last century. Further on there is a tiny neo-classical chapel.

Historians and architects should enjoy seeing the fine *buffet d'eau.*

JARDIN DES PLANTES, MONTPELLIER
163 Rue Auguste Broussonnet, 34000 Montpellier.

*North west of the town centre, just north of the Promenade de Peyrou and the Arc de Triomphe. Easy to find, but the one-way system makes parking nearby difficult. (156 C3)* **Opening hours:** *April to October, 8.30-12 and 2-6; November to March, 8-12 and 2-5.30. Closed Sundays and holidays. E. Free. Wheelchairs.*

The original Jardin des Plantes was created at the end of the sixteenth century and is the oldest botanic garden in France. It was destroyed by

Cardinal Richelieu in 1622 and a smaller version was remade but lost its importance with the creation of the Paris Jardin des Plantes in 1626.

The plant order beds, with their collection of native wild flowers, are in front of the orangery and there are also glasshouses and an arboretum, a water lily pond and a small rock garden. All the plants are well labelled. In the arboretum, there is an enormous *Parrotia persica* the size of a London plane, a *Phillyrea latifolia* dating from the seventeenth century, a *Zelkova serrata* and several lagerstroemias. The bamboo grove, with stems of yellow, black and glaucous green, is underplanted very effectively with glossy acanthus and ivy.

One of the interesting features is the mount, near the order beds, which was built with north and south facing terraces to provide separate microclimates for the plants. The small rock garden contains unusual varieties of some familiar species, *Echium pininana, Aquilegia canadensis, Erodium gruinum* and *Caccinia strigosa* a member of the borage family. Another unusual plant is the climber that grows near the orangery and looks like a wisteria. It is *Mucuna sempervirens* and has long racemes of dark, chestnut-purple flowers.

Also in Montpellier is the imposing **Promenade de Peyrou,** an eighteenth century promenade in the centre of the town. At one end is a fine, decorative iron gate while at the other, a pavilion has been built over the reservoir that is the end of a 9 km aqueduct. A grand statue of Louis XIV is another focus of this very eighteenth century ensemble of ranks of trees and broad walk.

## MIDI PYRENEES
Map: see page 128

### HAUTE GARONNE

JARDIN DES PLANTES, TOULOUSE
Allées F.Mistral or Allée J.Guesde, 31000 Toulouse.

*South of the cathedral. Take the D2, Direction Revel, and get ready to pull in after driving round the Grand Rond. The entrance is on the right of Allées F. Mistral. (152 C3)* **Opening hours:** *Every day 8-dusk. E. Free. Wheelchairs. Toilets.*

This is Toulouse's largest central public park and contains children's play areas, water features, ducks, peacocks, statues and bedding plants.

A row of pillar roses forms a pleasant feature and there are some magnificent trees including an enormous *Tilia tomentosa*. In addition to the ginkgo, blue cedar, taxodium and black walnut trees, there are also *Cladrastis lutea,* which has fragrant white flowers in long panicles in June, the uncommon

*Torreya nucifera, Picea glehnii, P. likiangensis* and a *Gymnocladus dioica*, (Kentucky coffee tree).

The Jardin des Plantes is attached by a bridge and a walkway to the garden on the **Grand Rond** and from there to the attractive **Jardin Royal**.

## HAUTES PYRENEES

JARDIN MASSEY
Rue Massey, 65000 Tarbes.

*North of the town centre, and on the same road as the main railway station but further east, across the D935 to Bordeaux. (168 C1)* **Opening hours:** *Every day from 7 or 8 until 6 in winter and 8 or 9 in summer. E. Free. Wheelchairs. Toilets.*

An attractive public park laid out by Placide Massey who was a gardener at St Cloud. When he retired, he returned to his native town where he created this botanic garden c.1850.

An avenue of palm trees and pillar roses leads from the entrance into the park where there are island beds of trees underplanted with shrubs. *Cedrus libani libani, Juglans nigra, Podocarpus neriifolius* and *Fagus sylvatica heterophylla* 'Asplenifolia', (fern-leafed beech), are some of the well-labelled trees that can be found.

Narrow curving rills take water all round the park, which is further enlivened by the crisp colors of mandarin ducks and the plaintive cries of the peacocks that wander freely about. A domed greenhouse contains a collection of exotic plants and there is a tiny cloister with carved capitals and a magnolia in the centre.

## TARN

PALAIS DE LA BERBIE
Place de l'Eglise Sainte-Cécile, 81000 Albi.

*Behind the Musée d'Art Contemporain and the Toulouse Lautrec collection which is near Albi's breathtaking brick cathedral. (153 F1)* **Opening hours:** *Every day from 9-6. E. Free. Toilets inside the museum, for which there is a charge.*

A fine example of a *parterre en broderie* in the small walled garden between the Palais and the river Tarn. It won first prize as a *'monument historiques fleuris'* in 1993. Crozier shapes of clipped box are framed by a border of bedding plants, while foliage plants like the deep red iresine form the design of the central rondel.

There are shrub borders at each end, hydrangeas along the wall of the Palais and climbing roses trained up the wall on the river side. This wall has a walkway along the top, shaded by a vine-covered pergola, from where there is a splendid view of the *parterre*, the two bridges over the Tarn and the soft pink brick buildings that crowd the opposite bank. The walk has niches in it with statues and an attractive pavilion at one end.

Also in Albi is the **Parc Rochegude** (Boulevard Carnot, south of the town, where the roads from Toulouse and Castres converge.) After the immaculate condition of the award-winning *parterre en broderie* at the Palais de Berbie, Rochegude is disappointing. A program of restoration is to start shortly.

JARDIN DE L'EVECHE
81100 Castres.

*In front of the Hotel de Ville (which also houses the Musée Goya), on the west bank of the river Agoût. Parking near the Cathedral of St Benoit. (154 A3)* **Opening hours:** *All the time. E. Free. Wheelchairs. Toilets opposite.*

The fine *parterre en broderie* was designed by Le Nôtre and was carried out in the last years of the seventeenth century. The box of the period in the form of fantastic arabesques and Prince of Wales plumes against gravel are surrounded by a double border with bright bedding plants and drums, domes and lollipops of clipped yew. Beyond the two oblong *parterres*, four simpler beds surround a pool and fountain. Clipped limes and chestnuts form a background to the garden. Although the box hedges have grown rather too large, because of their age they cannot be cut too closely. However, the *parterre* is still one of the finest examples of its kind.

PARC DE FOUCAUD
81600 Gaillac. Tel: 63 57 00 37 (Mairie de Gaillac).

*On the edge of the town, on the D964 to Graulhet. (153 E1)* **Opening hours:** *Every day 8-sunset. E. Free. Wheelchairs, only to the garden in front of the château. Toilets.*

The garden in front of the Château de Gaillac is as severely classical as the brick façade of the château itself, with regular lines of limes, rectangular lawns and an area for boules. In a direct line with the lawn, facing the château, are the *communs* or outbuildings. Unusually, these are in a 'Palladian rustic' style with the front forming a semicircle.

At the back however, the garden is in the Italian style and descends in terraces to the river Tarn. It has pools, fountains and small waterfalls, box-edged *parterres* and drums of clipped box. A charming small pavilion with a statue of Neptune on top, has a *salle fraiche* or cool room with four niches inside and dates from the beginning of the seventeenth century.

A small section of the park, to the west, is a contemporary flower garden, with shrubs and roses.

## CHATEAU DE ST GERY
81800 Rabastens. Tel: 63 33 70 43.

*40 km from Toulouse and Albi and south-west of Gaillac. Turn south off the N88, midway between Rabastens and Lisle-sur-Tarn. (153 E2)* **Opening hours:** *1 July to 31 August, every day 2-6; Easter to All Saints, Sundays and holidays 2-6.30. E. Moderate, includes château. Wheelchairs. Toilets in château.*

The château, built of the soft red brick of the area in the fourteenth century and remodelled in the fifteenth has been described as looking like a north Italian palazzo. The *cour d'honneur* is guarded by two fine *sphinges* (female sphinxes) on low walls and the whole is surrounded by a park.

It is natural and unspoiled. Robinias and Judas trees mix with horse chestnuts, field maples and hornbeams. Here, there is a classical urn, there a terracotta statue of a Madonna and child. The statue overlooks an empty *bassin*, a basket of fruit on a pedestal in the middle and wild poppies growing through cracks. Corn and vines from the surrounding farm land encroach into the garden.

There is a particularly attractive orangery that was built in 1785, which makes it one of the last to be erected before the Revolution. Nearby a fountain flows from beneath a mediaeval stone carved with the arms of the Seigneur of St Géry.

The château terrace overlooks the river Tarn with a view of the weir in one direction and an aqueduct in the other. This is not a grand, or even a highly gardened garden but one in which to wander about making discoveries.

# GLOSSARY

Several French terms are used in this guide because an exact translation is cumbersome: the English ' alley', for example, is a narrow passage between buildings and not the dignified, tree-lined walk signified by ' allée'.

**allée**   walk or avenue with plants or trees on either side.

**bas-relief**  sculpture carved out of a basically flat surface against which the figures stand out only a little.

**bassin**   small formal pool, usually in stone.

**bosquet**   grove or shrubbery.

**boulingrin**  corruption of 'bowling green'. A sunken lawn.

**buffet d'eau**   architectural feature placed against a wall or niche, with water flowing over it.

**cour d'honneur**   the principal courtyard where guests are received.

**fabrique**   a very useful term which covers garden constructions including temples, columns, grottoes, pavilions, arches etc.

**grille d'honneur**   Elaborate main gate made from wrought iron bars.

**haut-relief**   sculpture carved from a flat surface, where the figures stand out clear of the background.

**miroir d'eau**   large formal pool designed to be a reflecting surface, usually to reflect the château.

**nymphée**   grotto.

**parterre**   flat, ornamental area often near the house or château; may have flowers or be turf cut in geometric patterns with gravel paths.

**parterre en broderie**   elaborate and flowing design with box hedges.

**pièce d'eau**   formal pool, probably of stone. Larger than a *bassin*.

**plan d'eau**   sheet of water, larger than a pond but not a lake.

**potager**   vegetable garden.

**solitude**   small, enclosed bower.

# Index

169

## Acknowledgements

The photographer, Deirdre Hall, and I would like to thank all the owners, conservateurs and officials in France who have shown us round and answered questions, the Stena Sealink Line Newhaven-Dieppe for many trouble-free channel crossings and Christopher Helm publishers who first commissioned this book.

Deirdre Hall and Susan Rowland must take all the credit for the visual aspects of this book. Any faults are mine alone. I would also like to thank Miranda Abbs, Stewart Ferguson, Gisèle and Dominique Grant, Bron Grilleo, Virginia Hinze, Gillian Mawrey, Michelle Pavitt, J. Ramsbotham, and Tony Thorlby for all their help. An especial thank you to Susan Rowland, Mark Le Fanu and the Society of Authors and, of course, to Peter Abbs who held the fort while I was away and has made many invaluable suggestions and given me constant support.

Order copies from:

Sagapress, Inc.
P.O. Box 21
Sagaponack, NY 11962
Fax: (516) 537-5415